D0282930

You are a Contender!

You are a Contender!

Build Emotional Muscle to Perform Better and
Achieve More ... in Business, Sports and Life

John Haime

New York

You are a Contender!

Build Emotional Muscle to Perform Better and
Achieve More ... in Business, Sports and Life

Copyright © 2010 John Haime. All rights reserved.

No part of this publication may be reproduced or transmitted in any form or by any means, mechanical or electronic, including photocopying and recording, or by any information storage and retrieval system, without permission in writing from the author or publisher (except by a reviewer, who may quote brief passages and/or short brief video clips in a review.)

Disclaimer: The Publisher and the Author make no representations or warranties with respect to the accuracy or completeness of the contents of this work and specifically disclaim all warranties, including without limitation warranties of fitness for a particular purpose. No warranty may be created or extended by sales or promotional materials. The advice and strategies contained herein may not be suitable for every situation. This work is sold with the understanding that the Publisher is not engaged in rendering legal, accounting, or other professional services. If professional assistance is required, the services of a competent professional person should be sought. Neither the Publisher nor the Author shall be liable for damages arising herefrom. The fact that an organization or website is referred to in this work as a citation and/or a potential source of further information does not mean that the Author or the Publisher endorses the information the organization or website may provide or recommendations it may make. Further, readers should be aware that internet websites listed in this work may have changed or disappeared between when this work was written and when it is read.

Cover art by Paul Edwards Design

ISBN 978-1-60037-686-3

Library of Congress Control Number: 2009932817

MORGAN · JAMES
THE ENTREPRENEURIAL PUBLISHER

Morgan James Publishing, LLC
1225 Franklin Ave., STE 325
Garden City, NY 11530-1693
Toll Free 800-485-4943
www.MorganJamesPublishing.com

In an effort to support local communities, raise awareness and funds, Morgan James Publishing donates one percent of all book sales for the life of each book to Habitat for Humanity. Get involved today, visit www.HelpHabitatForHumanity.org.

Acknowledgments

So many people are responsible for giving me the ability to give back. My parents, Dawn and Peter Haime, set the groundwork for my journey by providing a solid base of emotional stability during my early years. Their ongoing support is appreciated. Thanks also to Kevin, Lisa, Jake and Jackson for your support.

To Tricia and Aidan—you're the best and your great support and strength to keep me going is appreciated.

Special thanks to Robyn Spizman for getting this process started. Robyn lit the fire and made sure that I followed through.

Joanne Godin has done a remarkable job as an advisor. Her ideas, skilful editing and writing expertise were a big factor in making this project successful.

Paul Edwards added a great deal to the book by bringing ideas to life through his graphic talent.

Thank you to Scott Spreier and Bill Tredwell of The Hay Group for your thoughts and ideas.

Thanks to Izzy Justice of EQmentor for the enlightening conversations.

Thank you to Martyn Newman for agreeing to write the book's foreword. Martyn is a world-class expert in his field and provided great insights. I look forward to further collaboration. I would also like to thank John Broderick, Martyn's RocheMartin colleague in Ireland.

Many thanks to my great readers: Eric Kaufmanis, Chris Fitzgerald, Dana Tierney and Paul Lebreux who read with interest and provided feedback.

Special thanks to Angelo Boy, who contributed to my thinking on a number of areas of the book.

Working with the very capable team at Morgan James, especially my Author Relations Manager, Margo Toulouse, has been a great experience.

Thank you all for your valuable contributions.

Foreword

How do the world's best athletes and performers make it to the top and stay there? Talent and skill are not enough in themselves. Emotions run the show in elite performance.

To produce outstanding achievement in any sport, talent and skill are essential elements that get you in the game. But, once you're in the game, recent research in sports psychology has identified another set of factors that control the outcome. Athletes who have learned a particular set of skills to manage their emotions intelligently produce consistently superior performance.

Collectively these skills are referred to as emotional intelligence (EQ) and it's EQ that determines whether you are mentally tough enough to remain self-motivated and sustain your competitive energy; whether you can take emotional control in response to frustration and disappointment; whether you can stay mentally alert and focused to deal with distractions and stress; and whether you can maintain the power of purpose that enables you to reach beyond your current limits and attain your highest goals.

Emotions really are the engine in the vehicle of performance, and the skills associated with using emotions intelligently are indispensible to achieving competitive advantage for elite performers. In this book, You Are a Contender! Build Emotional Muscle to Perform Better and Achieve More ... in Business, Sports and Life, John Haime has done a remarkable job of highlighting the key attribute of all effective performance—self-awareness. Becoming self-aware in a skilful way enables you to know yourself and your motivations and allows you to tap into those internal resources that make your talent dance.

I have been working with leaders in organizations worldwide for the past fifteen years. From my work with emotional intelligence and the Emotional Capitalist model, it is very clear to me that the skills that separate average performers from star performers are grounded in the ability to be self-aware. What is true of high performers in the corporate world is also true of top performers in the world of elite sport.

In recent years we have conducted extensive research in Europe and Asia using the Emotional Intelligence Sports Inventory (EQSi)—the world's first scientific tool specifically designed to measure emotional intelligence and sports performance. The EQSi has identified the key performance indicators that separate average and elite professional and top amateur athletes. Once again, the data demonstrates that self-awareness is the platform upon which the indispensible skills of emotional intelligence are built.

John's book reaches the same conclusion, but from the perspective of a practitioner. John's rare combination of skills, having played a professional sport at a world-class level, his work with top organizations and world-class performers and his engaging writing style make this book informative, practical and entertaining. While this book is filled with great information, it is not academic. It is packed with psychological insights and techniques that the reader can use immediately to improve performance and overcome those persistent errors that sabotage skill execution. The tone of the book comes from someone who feels what the reader does. John has had many ups and downs in his journey and has had close, first-hand connection with some of the world's top performers and coaches. These experiences provide compelling illustrations of the power of emotions in all performance. The reader will immediately recognize many similar challenges in their own performance and gain new and valuable insights for overcoming common setbacks.

I wholeheartedly recommend You Are a Contender! Build Emotional Muscle to Perform Better and Achieve More ... in Business, Sports and Life, as a book that is long overdue. Personally, I am looking forward to working with John and his group to bring his message as well as the Emotional Intelligence Sports Inventory to coaches and athletes around the world. In the meantime, read this book today, commit to the ideas and practice the skills. I am confident that John has given us a roadmap to take personal and professional performance to the next level.

Martyn Newman, PhD, DPsych
President, RocheMartin
Author, Emotional Capitalists: The New Leaders
Melbourne, Australia

Contents

Introduction: More, better, always!

Since 1997 I have had the privilege of working with world-class corporate leaders, athletes and others, using my experience as a tournament professional golfer and accreditations as a coach in the areas of performance and leadership, to help people create a clear path to where they want to go. Much of my work has to do with helping individuals get out of their own way. It seems no matter where I go, and in what area of performance, people tell me they are seeking the same things: "I'd like to achieve more," and "I'd just like to be more consistent."

This book evolved from the overwhelming number of requests and suggestions I have received in my speaking engagements around the world over the past two years. I have been strongly encouraged to write a book and share some practical information with you. So here it is.

My background is in professional golf but you don't have to be a golfer to read this book. The performance lessons and parallels I will introduce you to are applicable to everything you do. Since golf is a difficult, frustrating, emotional game played on a surface with rewards and penalties, it really does reflect our experiences on the surfaces we are playing on every day. In my work with world-class performers in business, leadership and sports, I have found many of the lessons transferable.

Garry Jacobs, author of The Vital Difference, said it best. Writing about the golf movie Bagger Vance, where a prodigy golfer, Randolph Junah, wins a tournament after learning about himself, with the help of his mentor, a wise, mystical caddie named Bagger Vance:

> Some readers may think that this is only a story about a game. It is not real life and it is not about serious accomplishment. Bagger's message is that all life is a game, the play of the Divine lila. Running a family or a business or running for office are only various expressions of the game.

My work has been telling people the truth about what they need to do to help themselves, highlighting things that hinder consistent performance, and creating a plan to modify their behaviors. This book is not about quick tricks and tips or fast fixes that aren't sustainable. Instead, it provides a mirror to see yourself as you are and helps you build the emotional muscle you need to deal with the experiences and challenges in your life and in the life you want to lead. It will require a committed effort from you.

What might be holding you back from being a consistent performer in areas of your life? Whether you're leading a business, your family, your community group, or playing golf or any activity you love; whether you're playing at the level of the Fortune 100 or the PGA, running your own startup, or playing your favorite activity on the weekends; the answer to these questions lies within reach. The answer, simply put, is a deeper understanding of your behavior and why you tend to do the things you do in the office, on the job, at home, on the playing field or on the golf course. Once you learn that, you can quickly learn to manage your behavior more to your advantage. Everything starts with you.

Perhaps you have already heard or read some things that sound like this. After all, everyone knows that people perform better when they play within themselves, when they're in the zone. So, if it's such common knowledge, what's keeping you out of that zone so much of the time?

I'd like the opportunity to show you how to be better prepared to deal with the experiences in your life. This will help you improve your performances and become consistent. I'll show you what works for world-class performers and what has worked with some of our world-class clients. What separates contenders from pretenders and what makes one person a one-hit-wonder and another able to create consistent, sustainable results?

The keys are self-awareness and management of emotions. I'll help you test yourself to see if you are aware of your own behaviors and tendencies, and whether you are able to manage your emotions when it counts. Since most—80%—of the people I test are not self-aware, I'll give you the tools you need to get to the place that opens doors to greater achievement and consistency in your life.

A note to all athletes

If you believe that managing emotion through self-awareness is only important in those endeavors that provide lots of time to think about things—like golf—and not in high speed reaction sports like football, basketball, soccer, cricket, rugby, baseball, hockey, skiing and others, my experience working with performers says otherwise.

Most sports, and you can name almost all of them, have more down time than actual playing time—and this is where the heart and mind have to be conditioned to let your talent come out. For example, most athletes spend hours getting ready for the game. This is when the emotions have an opportunity to impact the player's state of mind and influence his or her emotional state later, during the game. In the National Football League, only 12 out of 60 game minutes are actually spent playing the game. There's lots of opportunity in the other 48 for disruptive negative emotions and clouded thinking to have an impact on the 12 minutes the player is engaging in action.

In one of the world's fastest reaction games, ice hockey, players prepare hours before a hockey game and play 60 minutes, with the average player on the ice for only 15 to 25 minutes. The rest of the time is spent watching, waiting and preparing. In the 2006 Stanley Cup Playoffs, when the favored Ottawa Senators lost to the Buffalo Sabres, the Sabres' centre Daniel Brière explained the difference between the two teams under the pressures of the situation:

> "I think we stayed in control of our emotions during the key times better than them, and I think that was the difference. It's not that we outplayed them; I just think we found more composure at key moments of the games."

I have hundreds of quotes from athletes in all sports identifying the ability to manage their emotions as a major key for them in winning.

With advances and improvements in all aspects of sport, including training methods, coaching and video technology, it becomes more and more difficult for an athlete to stand out from others. It takes more effort and it takes something else to set one individual apart from others in performance. Every athlete has the ability to become bigger, stronger, faster and more technically sound. Self-awareness—with the core ability to direct yourself under pressure when it counts—is one of the few remaining ways you can differentiate a contender from a pretender.

I can confidently tell you that without a deep belief in yourself, consistent, sustainable performance is not realistic. Self-awareness is the key to you believing in yourself. And, I mean 100 percent committed to yourself and what you are doing. Every inch of you has to believe that the goals you have set for yourself are achievable and that there is no doubt they will be achieved. They may be modified or shaped as you work to reach them, but you will reach your goals.

The bottom line is that with self-awareness you have something you know and someone you understand to believe in—you. Without self-awareness, you are attempting to believe in something and someone that you don't truly know and understand, so the belief is not genuine. This is the cruel reality for many performers.

Wherever the top is for you—in your career, your family, your friendships, your passion—it often comes down to a single, defining opportunity that makes the difference between achievement and failure. That is the moment when you need to pull it all together. This book will take you on a journey that can shift your career, enhance your life and make you a contender in everything you do.

1   What drives you?

"Tennis, running, and golf: depending on whether
I want to abuse my elbows, my knees, or my emotions."

Phil Knight
Chairman, President and CEO of Nike Inc.,
when asked about his passions outside work

I have always been fascinated by performance and what separates the average from the outstanding. My own tournament professional golf career ignited a curiosity to understand how a world-class golfer couldn't reach his potential and, perhaps more importantly, be frustrated and miserable much of the time. And I know I am not alone. Many who reach for the stars fall to the earth scratching their heads and looking for answers.

My search has taken me on a big journey, from great education, through personal experience in top-level international competition, to working with the best in their fields and having the opportunity to ask about and understand what they do.

We are all performers in life. Whether you know it or not, if you're leading, working, parenting, creating and developing a relationship, playing golf or enjoying your passion, you are on stage. And along with performance comes pressure, in varying degrees. How we handle the pressure usually determines if we fly or fall down.

Like you, I have both flown and fallen down ... often. Let me share a time with you when I was under great pressure, how I felt, how I dealt with it, and the result.

My story—the disaster down under

I sat slumped on the end of my golf bag in Melbourne, Australia after missing the cut and losing another opportunity in professional golf. I was struggling and panic was setting in. I was frustrated, my sponsors were losing hope, and the future was not bright.

All I could think about was that I seemed to be getting worse instead of better. How could this happen? What was I doing wrong? Was I that bad? Where was the talent that had gotten me to this point?

As usual I headed for the practice area where, with no pressure, I hit ball after ball straight and long—a normal result after struggling when it counted. It certainly wasn't my technique causing all of the grief ... it was more than that.

My downward spiral had started weeks earlier, at another international tournament, when the world's top golfer at the time, Australia's Greg Norman, changed the dynamic of my world. The atmosphere became charged when the world's number one golfer showed up to play in a tournament. There was more money, more people, more pressure. This event stands out more than any other in a disappointing career. I was an unproven twenty-two-year-old with an opportunity to prove myself on the world stage and gain some momentum in what was supposed to be a promising future in professional golf.

I stood on the first tee in Melbourne, waiting to hit my opening shot in front of thousands of golf fans. The people were waiting for their hero, who as fate would have it, was playing in the group behind me. I felt small and overwhelmed by the situation. Five minutes earlier, as I had warmed up next to the tee area, I had felt my hands and knees shaking for the first time in my life. I was warming up inches away from the world's number one golfer—and he looked bigger than life!

The first few holes were terribly uncomfortable. I had been playing golf since the age of five, but had the feeling I had never played before. As I made my way to the final holes, the day was becoming more miserable as my score and head both spun out of control. The torture was almost over but not without a final freefall down the eighteenth hole.

I hit a long, straight drive off the eighteenth tee and I'm really not sure to this day how I did that with the range of emotions raging through me and throwing me off balance. There was a sea of people lining the fairway from the tee to the green to catch a glimpse of Mr. Norman, just behind. I was very much aware that the crowd was not there to see me.

My second shot wasn't difficult but it felt like the hardest shot in the world with thousands of impatient faces waiting for me to get on with it and get out of the way. My caddie suggested a 3-iron as a pretty good wind blew in our faces and the shot approached 200 yards. I agreed. A 3-iron it was. Greg was now on the eighteenth tee staring down the fairway at our group.

I set up as usual for the shot, looked at my target and down at my ball, swung my club and screamed a low, wild shot right into the crowd, hitting an older gentleman squarely on the shoulder.

The crowd cleared and made room for me to approach my next shot, an easy little 60 yarder I've hit a million times.

With my head in a dizzying frenzy, I swung the club back and delivered what was supposed to be a simple little shot onto the green, out over to the other side of the green and into the grandstand, hitting a middle-aged lady in the leg.

As I crossed to the other side of the green, the crowd, some of whom had been drinking beer all afternoon in the hot Australian sun, made it clear that I was a fly in the ointment. "Are you done, mate?" screamed one fan from the top of the grandstand. The big crowd's patience was thinning as their hero was now within view.

I dropped my ball away from the grandstand and proceeded to take five more clumsy shots before the agony ended. Feeling about an inch tall, I calculated my score, signed the official scorecard, and found a quiet spot to sit down and try and make sense of what had just happened.

My professional golf career continued on a similar path of mediocrity until the decision was made to wave the white flag. What was to have been a very promising professional golf career turned into five and a half years of inconsistent results, underachievement, frustration and headaches. There were some great moments and some achievement, but I couldn't seem to repeat it and create consistent results.

I had no idea then what happened, but after lots of reflection I have a very good idea now.

Fear, frustration, hesitation, panic and anger set the tone for my performance. As leading Emotional Intelligence expert Daniel Goleman outlines in his book Social Intelligence, I was frazzled. I was consistently knocked off my focus by negative emotions, and I didn't have the tools or knowledge to do something about it. These emotions shaped my thinking, which shaped my behavior, which shaped my performance. I worked hard and felt like I was practicing the right things but no amount of time at the practice range was going to reverse the downward spiral.

Feeling the heat

Do you feel pressure in your life? How do you deal with it?

When things aren't going as expected in the family, are you a prisoner to your emotions? When the economy slips and financial pressures fall on your shoulders, do you feel highly stressed?

When an important presentation at work must be delivered with persuasiveness and confidence, is your mind clear or cloudy?

When your boss is not handling the pressure well and is unfair, do you rise above it or let it ruin your day?

When you take on too much in your life, and you're juggling four things at once but only have time for three, do you feel strained and anxious? Simply, when the pressure is on in your life, do you rise to the occasion and play big with confidence and composure, or do you crumble and play small with fear?

Nowhere is the separator between pretenders and contenders clearer than at a professional golf event. The bigger the event, the bigger the gap of separation you will see between the top and bottom.

One of the biggest events in professional golf is The Masters tournament played each April in Augusta, GA. It's the granddaddy. The best golfers on the planet arrive at Augusta to compete for the green jacket and the prize money. The world's media cover the event and golf fans everywhere watch, as it officially starts the golf season.

For the past few years, I have visited The Masters with a group of people to watch the practice sessions on Monday and Tuesday. Part of the fun of the experience is for each of us to predict the winner. We watch the players hit long shots on the practice tee, tune up their putting on the practice green, fine tune their touch with shorter shots around the green, and practice on the course to get a feel for the variety of shots they'll need to hit in the real rounds. Each of us then chooses, based on what we see, who we think will win. Now remember here, we watch the practice rounds and not the real thing. The actual event begins on Thursday and finishes up on Sunday afternoon.

I can confidently tell you that every player we watch in the practice sessions looks fantastic. Most are in good form and are peaking for the event. They hit the ball long and straight on the practice tee, roll the ball nicely on the practice green, and the relaxed atmosphere produces some great shot making.

We have found that it is virtually impossible, based on the practice sessions, to predict who will do well and who won't. In fact, we're always surprised how far down the list our picks are when we get the final results on Sunday afternoon. After playing professional golf and knowing something about the game, you'd think I would be able to separate the good talent from the great. But in our little competition, I really don't do very well!

So what does this mean?

When players, leaders and performers in general are under pressures in dynamic, changing environments funny things happen and behavior changes. The Masters tournament for professional golfers is the ultimate pressure test, where the pressure intensifies each day from Thursday through Sunday, and only those equipped to handle it flourish. For many, the great talent seen in the practice sessions on Monday and Tuesday shrinks—big talent suddenly becomes small. The calm, clear, relaxed demeanor earlier in the week turns anxious and cloudy as the week goes on. Each day the pressure grows. The players get closer to the grand prize and the rewards that come with it; they are pushed to their limits and the distractions increase. Those able to deal with these pressures will contend, those who can't, won't.

The same general principle applies if you attend a conference with a number of CEOs addressing an audience. Watching and listening to them speak, try picking the CEOs that are running highly successful companies and which ones are leading companies that are just making the cut. No matter how impressive they sound in this environment, unless you can observe the CEOs in their dynamic, changing environments, making decisions under day to day pressures in the competitive business environment, it is very difficult to assess whether they are consistent, sustainable performers.

Contenders and pretenders will often look the same to you or me, but they are very different. A contender is an authentic individual who can sustain performance over time. A contender is consistent. A pretender is an actor that struggles to repeat performance. Here are a few key ways that pretenders and contenders are different:

Contenders:	Pretenders:
Gobble up pressure	Are gobbled up by pressure
Are comfortable in their own skin	Are not quite comfortable
Connect with their core values and live them	Constantly change their values to meet new needs and situations
Are proactive	Are reactive
Look in the mirror and change what they don't like	Avoid the mirror and stay the same
Create impressions that last over time	Create great first impressions but are unable to sustain a lasting impression
Ask others for their opinion on their performance	Rely on their own, biased view of themselves
Commit to long-term improvement	Use band-aid fixes for short-term gain
Write down specific goals and commit to them	Create loose goals that don't require absolute commitment
Are courageous and confident	Are prisoners to fear
Are disciplined	Lack control
Play to their own standards	Play to meet others' expectations

Emotions drive people—people drive performance

It has become clear to me through my own experience and in my work with all levels of performers, that what really stops people from doing what they already know how to do is their failure to recognize the impact that emotions have on their actions and performance.

This becomes apparent when they cannot apply their everyday skills and knowledge under challenging or stressful situations.

The best of the best recognize the importance of this emotional intelligence, not only in realizing their potential but in sustaining it over time. The world's best golfer, Tiger Woods, tells reporters that controlling emotion is the key to winning professional golf championships. Former General Electric CEO Jack Welch made a similar observation about the importance of emotional control in the business world. He said:

> "Emotional intelligence is more rare than book smarts, but my experience says it is actually more important in the making of a leader—you just can't ignore it."

And broadcasters typically tell us before the final game in a playoff series or tournament that "If he/she/they can control their emotions today, they can win." This implies that if they don't have a handle on their emotions, they can't win. Very telling.

We all know that technical skills are critical to success in any endeavor. Being smart is important too. But, we know through research that intelligence is not the separator between pretenders and contenders. While great technique and knowledge about a subject will get you so far, the ability to be aware of your emotions and manage your responses under pressure is the differentiator.

My work with business people, leaders, athletes and others has shown me that being in tune with emotions is a critical piece in becoming a contender. We process and connect with the world through our emotions. More than two decades of research done by experts like Daniel Goleman and others in the field of emotional intelligence supports this finding. It shows that intelligence about emotions is twice as important as technical competence and IQ combined in determining whether someone's performance will be outstanding or average.

Goleman et al also tell us that we feel things before we think about them. It's important for you to know this order. It means that:

> Your emotions influence your thinking.
> Your thinking influences your behavior.
> Your behavior influences your performance.

The starting point in this chain, emotions, is what ensures clear thinking, positive behavior and the resulting consistent performance.

Emotions drive people and people drive performance.

Don't feel bad about not knowing about this or how important it is to you. We all follow similar paths in our lives. The first and most important thing in our lives is school. We are exhorted to study hard, learn as much as we can, perform as well as possible. Technical skills are the focus of our education and we are measured according to how much we know. There is no systematic approach to teaching us how to handle ourselves under pressure, how to become self-aware, and how to create consistent, sustainable relationships. These things simply are not part of the curriculum. It is left up to us to develop these skills on our own in the schoolyard, on the playing field, at the office and at home.

What's ahead?

My mission for the remainder of the book is to introduce you to the keys that will help you become a contender more often. I'll introduce you to some of the world's top performers, like golfer Tiger Woods and business leader Bill George, and you'll see what they do to stay on top. You'll read about the Emotional Peak and Emotional Wedge, and how your background can influence where you are now. You'll learn about the emotional spiral and how it works. I'd also like you to complete your own emotional inventory and learn about how emotional memories can impact your game today. I'll assign you your own, personal, emotional caddie who will guide you and help you become a more consistent performer. All of these ideas will help you climb the leaderboard in your own life. Athletes know that if they are on the leaderboard, a board showing the rankings of the leaders in a competition, they are in contention. I want you to get on the leaderboard in your life … and stay there.

To climb the leaderboard, an understanding of you is the key. Let's have a look at where and how you started and what that means to your performance … in everything you do.

2 How solid is your base?

"It is often tragic to see how blatantly a man bungles his own life and the lives of others yet remains totally incapable of seeing how much the whole tragedy originates in himself, and how he continually feeds it and keeps it going."

Carl Jung
Swiss Psychiatrist

In my professional golf career, I travelled the world. Each time I arrived in a strange city where I didn't know anyone, I would head to the golf course, where everything seemed familiar, to begin practice for the week. The first thing I would do is talk to the Caddie Master, the person responsible for assigning a caddie to each of the professional players. The caddie carried my clubs and generally looked after my golf needs for the week. Because the name John Haime was not well-known and I was not one of the top-ranked players in the world, I usually had someone assigned to me, a local golfer volunteering for the week.

I don't remember many of my caddies through the years. Most just carried the clubs and didn't add much to my success or failure. But I do remember one gentleman

named Brian who caddied for me in Victoria, British
Columbia, Canada. He actually met me in the parking
lot the moment I arrived at the tournament, introduced
himself and proceeded to take my clubs and shoes so I
could focus on checking in and getting organized for
the day's practice session. As soon as I met him, I knew
there was something different about this caddie. He was
helping me and was really interested in me as a golfer,
and I hadn't even hit a shot yet!

Consistent performers know where they come from and
understand how their experiences impact their performance today
and every day. Inconsistent performers may not understand how
their past experiences throw them off balance. They may rely on
quick fixes to temporarily cover up deeper problems.

My experience after playing a professional sport and working
with many different types of performers in business and sports
is that you have to look at the big picture and go to the root
cause of a poor result before starting on the path to positive,
sustainable results. I have found with performers—whether they
are athletes, business people or other leaders—that popping a
positive thought in the mind and letting talent take over may
work in the short term, but it isn't sustainable. Looking at the
whole person and understanding their experiences—where they
come from—is the only way to help performers rid themselves
of damaging, negative emotions that emerge when the pressure is
cranked up. Once these emotions are recognized and understood,
a freedom in performance is possible where negative feelings are
replaced with positive ones. Until then, those negative feelings of

uncertainty that inexplicably appear when a great performance is needed will throw things off balance. This is true for top performers and it is true for you.

I admit it would be easier for you to invest in emotional cosmetic surgery and hope that it will cover up the warts that all of us are so intent to hide from view. To be frank, when things are going well and life is smooth for you, this type of surgery may work. But when things become difficult and uncomfortable, cosmetic surgery is never enough.

Quick fix = no fix

I was always curious as to why, when I played professional golf, advice like "Think more positively" or "Focus!" or "Block out distractions" never lasted. This advice to get my mind on the task would last for a short period of time and then I would be back in the same boat ... and I would find that the boat was still leaking! These tools to top performance were pointless without emotional composure and awareness.

I can't tell you how many times in my workshops and coaching people ask how to get rid of negative thinking. They are waiting for a simple fix that will magically make them think positively and see the world in a different way. I have to tell them that only when they understand what is causing their negative thinking, and explore their emotional memory for the negative experiences that fuel those negative thoughts, can they help themselves.

Being a contender in your life follows a similar principal. While cosmetic masking may make you feel good for a while, the feeling will fade and life will return to the same state it was when you began. You can try ideas like thinking positive, and spend endless hours tinkering and re-tinkering with your technical skills, or you can look at the root cause of why you aren't contending as often as you'd like and do the work toward a better performance and life.

Where do *you* come from?

How much does your background and the emotional environment you came from impact your life today? When researchers and some authors look at the best performers today, and what makes them tick, there is usually little focus on the performer's background. But this is where a person's emotional make-up is developed; it shapes the path that a person takes through life. While you can shape and change some things along the way—like getting a great education, for example—where you started can determine to a great extent where you end up.

I developed The Emotional Peak and The Emotional Wedge as models to demonstrate the impact that your starting point in life and your core emotional stability can have on the course of your life. You may not know the power and consequences that early emotional development has on different areas of your life. The diagrams show you how initial positive or negative experiences re-emerge throughout your life and alter the experiences of work, school, relationships and community life. While the models highlight the extremes of emotional stability and instability, each of us, to some degree, will fit more into one or the other of these models. It is also possible that we will shift between them at defining moments in our lives.

The Emotional Peak

Figure 2-1, The Emotional Peak, highlights a rich, positive, proactive path in life if emotional stability is the foundation. This model represents a deepening positive richness in a person's life as they transition from a wide, stable base to the Peak at the top of the model.

Figure 2-1: The Emotional Peak

The key to this model is the base. The starting point is wide and solid, making emotional stability the defining feature of the Peak person's life. Early in life, positive emotional experiences and a stable, predictable environment encourage and help develop emotional stability. The range of positive emotional support can include great support from parents in whatever the young person chooses to do, a solid value system where parental actions align with the family's core values, parents who are self-aware themselves, and opportunities for the children to express their emotions. The consequences of this foundation are positive and a solid preparation for life's challenges.

I'm sure you recognize these features. You either had them in your life as a young person, or you may have had a friend who did. Whether it was your home or a friend's, it was a home that felt warm and welcoming. The parents asked you questions about how you were doing. The interaction among the members of the family was authentic. People laughed and expressed their emotions—positive and negative—and were encouraged to do so. Even negative emotions like anger are expressed and not suppressed in this kind of environment. It is just that the anger is managed, not out of control, and dealt with as an indication of a problem or issue that needs to be resolved.

This stable base sets up the opportunity for the young person in the Peak model to seek out and create positive, fulfilling relationships with people in their lives, including family, friends, coaches, spouse, children and others. This starting point is a very important stage in a person's life. Fulfilling and positive relationships at home help the person to create positive emotional experiences that are ingrained in their emotional memory, where each of us holds our positive and negative experiences and impressions. Throughout life, these emotional memories are the basis for our thinking, behavior and resulting performances. The Peak model creates a store of positive experiences in our emotional memory.

A Peak person is able to connect with others at work by being authentic and positive. He or she can inspire others, lead themselves and lead others. You know this person well. He or she is the boss or teacher or coach that was always in control, encouraged you when you needed a push, and showed empathy when you were down.

At the Peak of the model, the person takes on opportunities to give back to others and to their community … the ultimate achievement in a rich life. You know examples of people who have followed this path. They are contenders, proactive and consistent in everything they do. I have the opportunity to work with and coach people who fit the Peak profile. They all possess the same desire to give back to the community and those around them. There is a level of comfort and awareness of themselves. Because a Peak person knows who they are and where they are going, they have the space inside themselves to share their knowledge and experience with others.

There are many examples of contenders who give back great contributions to their communities. Corporate leaders often choose to share their knowledge by teaching in academic institutions following their careers. Some, like Microsoft founder Bill Gates, dedicate their lives to philanthropy and support worthwhile community causes. World-class athletes may coach others to reach higher achievement. The world's best golfer Tiger Woods created the Tiger Woods Learning Centre, a 35,000 square foot institution in Anaheim, CA for students in Grades 5-12.

The Emotional Wedge

There is also the chance that you experienced some elements of the emotional wedge as your starting environment.

Figure 2-2, The Emotional Wedge, is The Emotional Peak turned upside down. The Wedge is unstable because it is on a very small emotional base and therefore always teetering. The movement from the bottom of the model represents deepening emotional turmoil as a result of the emotional instability created in the person who experiences a Wedge environment. Emotional instability emerges from a number of factors, including a lack of support from parents, values that do not align with the parents' actions, a lack of self-awareness by the parents, a drive for surface achievements, and emotional suppression, whereby the young people are not encouraged to express feelings and are not asked about them.

You may recognize these features in your life or in the life of someone you knew as a young person. When you walked into the Wedge person's home, there was an uncomfortable feeling of emotional instability. Things may have been too perfect and not authentic, where nothing meaningful was ever said and behavior was superficial. Or, you were afraid to do or say anything for fear of a negative reaction, as people acted as though they were walking on eggshells.

You might also recognize the parents who promote surface achievements. They want their child to be successful, and create their own image of success for them. They want ribbons and trophies. They will have unreal perceptions of the child's talent, which is a burden on the child. They may push the child into something where there is no real sense of accomplishment for the child. The child may not be guided to the things they are most passionate about.

The instability at the bottom of this model wedges built-up negative emotion into relationships and work. A Wedge person does not seek deep, meaningful relationships. These are often superficial and squeezed into their schedules. The narrow base and unfulfilled relationships will carry into the work life where the Wedge person creates false appearances and artificial successes. The Wedge person may have difficulty keeping jobs and will be inconsistent in their performance. Negative emotions like fear, anxiety, insecurity and frustration are well established in the Wedge person's emotional memory. This translates into negative thinking, negative behavior and negative performance at work.

You know this person well too: a boss, coach or teacher who had trouble controlling their anger when the pressure was turned up, and who favored negative over positive feedback. When you spoke to them, you always got the feeling they weren't listening.

Because of negative emotional baggage and a cloudy mind, the Wedge person has little to give back. While the Peak allows for a person to be proactive and have plenty of room for sharing, the Wedge is reactive and closes the space for giving. The Wedge person is so caught up in their own internal dramas that there is little room for giving back. The giving space is filled by breakdowns, denial and inappropriate anger.

Figure 2-2: The Emotional Wedge

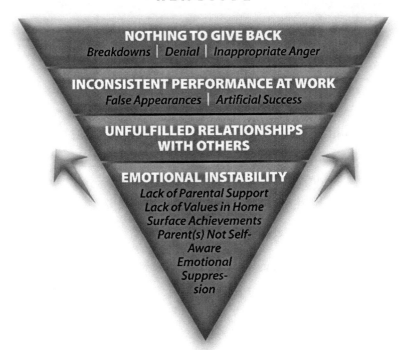

REACTIVE

NOTHING TO GIVE BACK
Breakdowns | Denial | Inappropriate Anger

INCONSISTENT PERFORMANCE AT WORK
False Appearances | Artificial Success

UNFULFILLED RELATIONSHIPS
WITH OTHERS

EMOTIONAL INSTABILITY
*Lack of Parental Support
Lack of Values in Home
Surface Achievements
Parent(s) Not Self-
Aware
Emotional
Suppres-
sion*

So what does this mean for you? Are you closer to the Peak path or the Wedge path? Or, is your starting point a combination of the two? Our circumstances as children, or at later stages of our lives can put us in the Wedge and hinder us from having the performance experiences of those who are in the Peak.

It is always your decision to break the cycle of the wedge. Part of breaking the cycle is not blaming parents or those coaches, teachers and others who had influence over you for their lack of self-awareness or their approach. Parents do the best they can given their circumstances and experience. An excellent example of this is in a statement by Tida Woods, the mother of Tiger Woods, who created a very stable platform for contender Tiger Woods, but did not have stability in her home as a young person, bouncing between two divorced parents who considered their later children more important than her. Quoted in an interview, she vowed, as a parent, that she would provide a stable environment for her child:

> "My father never hugged me or told me 'I love you.' So when I returned to Thailand from the U.S., I would hug him and say, 'I love you.' That's why I always hug Tiger and tell him I love him. Because I didn't have that."

Where you are in the Peak or the Wedge is your responsibility and the only person who can change the path between the two is you.

We all have unresolved emotions, some more than others. It is how we resolve those emotions that separates contenders from pretenders. Those who are self-aware will properly identify the unresolved emotions and learn to replace them—the highly negative ones—with positive ones. This gives you the opportunity to think clearly and make good decisions … and perform without the interference of powerful negative emotions. If the emotions remain unresolved, you are always open to them surprising you— often when you are under pressure and there is opportunity for them to be provoked. If you manage them, you can change your own thinking to provide positive support for your own efforts. We'll look at this more in depth in Chapter 6, The source of positive thinking.

Awareness is vital to you in everything you do. It is the key step in the creation process. With this book, you can begin the process of becoming self-aware so you will better understand why you feel what you feel, why you behave as you behave, and ultimately why you perform as you perform. You will then have the opportunity to identify areas you can build on and direct your life. The shift from pretender to contender begins with being self-aware. Let's look at the keys of self-awareness and the characteristics of people who are self-aware, a journey that starts with knowing who you really are.

3   Spiral up or spiral down

*"I think self-awareness is probably the most
important thing towards being a champion."*

Billie Jean King
Winner of 39 Grand Slam Tennis Titles

For my first practice session in Victoria, I headed for the first tee, ready to blast shots long and straight with my trusty driver. Instead, when I arrived, I saw my caddie Brian waving me over to the practice putting green, my putter and a ball in his hand.

"The first thing you'll need to understand is that these greens are a bit different John," he said. "You may want to spend most of your practice time this week on putting and learning how to handle those challenges."

That hadn't been my plan. I had wanted to practice my drives, which I knew were my strength. Instead, I was being told to focus on putting. Instead of feeling put out, however, I remember that it felt good having someone there who was looking after my interests and who knew what I needed. He was helping me in spite of myself.

> During the first day of practice, Brian asked a lot of questions, watched my shots carefully and talked to me about each hole, giving me insight on how to play each one. He stayed around after I played and we talked about the tournament. He had more ideas on how I could do well on the course.

Climbing the leaderboard is a metaphor of where we want to be in our lives. Pretenders seek the leaderboard, but can't quite get there. Contenders get on the board and their consistency enables them to stay there.

The first step in achieving consistent performance is identifying the need for improvement. We all need it, but do we all see that we need it? People who are self-aware are constantly identifying their need to change and improve. They know where to look and they ask themselves the following questions: Who am I? Where am I going? and How am I going to get there?

It all seems simple doesn't it? What could be so hard about mastering little old you? After all you're only one person. How difficult can it be to get a handle on only one person?

Ask most people and they will tell you that they have a pretty fair understanding of themselves and are in full control of what they are doing and where they are going. So then, why the need to go into all of this? The answer simply is that self-awareness is the fundamental piece that will help you become a consistent, sustained performer. A lack of it will keep you consistently out of reach of the achievement you seek ... in everything you do.

Building self-awareness is the key step

Self-awareness is the doorway to your life. It gives you the opportunity to access who you are at the deepest level and use that information to maximize your performance. The more I work with people on performance, helping them get to where they want to go, the more the importance of self-awareness is clear to me. The notes, calls and e-mails I receive from the people I work with make it clear they understand this key piece of the puzzle as they begin their journey to change their behavior. Here is a typical comment from a top performing participant in a Fortune 100 company, who participated in one my workshops: He recently wrote, "John, I am sure of one thing, performance is all about self-awareness. No improvement can occur until we learn to be self-aware."

That has been my experience. Without self-awareness, great performance is not possible. And you can't just go get it. It's not that simple. There are many facets to it and it involves everything you are as a person.

In my workshops, I have the opportunity to work with some tremendously talented and smart people who are often approaching the top of their field in business, industry and athletics. I see and assess their strengths, their limits and their overall capabilities. The process usually starts with some assessment tools to measure their competency in the behaviors characteristic of top performers. In the self-assessment, individuals simply answer questions about themselves. In the 360-degree feedback tool, their peers, bosses, friends, clients and others provide feedback on the individual's behavior. The 360-degree degree tool is much more revealing and interesting, as people get a broad perspective of their behavior and not just their own personal, biased view.

I enable my clients to find the truth about themselves in the gaps that show up between the way they see themselves and the way others see them. This starts them on the road to self-awareness.

Without self-awareness—the basic fundamental of emotional intelligence—I have found that more sophisticated behaviors are virtually impossible. A person with a lower level of self-awareness will struggle to develop consistent, sustainable relationships with others. A performer who has a low level of self-awareness will be unable to reach a consistent level of confidence and know their strengths, so they can play to them and adapt to challenging environments they find themselves in. It doesn't matter what the performance area is—whether it's business, sports, music, or performance in everyday life. If you lack self-awareness and some basic layers of emotional intelligence, you will struggle to be a consistent performer.

Spiral *into* control

In my workshops with corporate leaders and other performers, I use a model I developed to highlight the progressive nature of emotional intelligence. Each piece of the model—which is an element of emotional intelligence, starting with self-awareness— builds up to the next level or breaks down to the level below. In this way, a person can spiral up or spiral down, depending on their emotional state. I was originally introduced to this concept through a workshop I attended for golf professionals by golf instructors Pia Nilsson and Lynn Marriott. Nilsson is noted for her work with one of the all-time great players in women's golf, Annika Sorenstam, and is a pioneer in the highly successful Swedish golf program. As Nilsson and Marriott talked about how emotions impact golfers, their words resonated with me and I recalled my touring experiences.

Several years later, I developed The Emotional Spiral model, illustrating the impact of emotions on performance in a variety of areas, including business and leadership. It shows how emotions and emotional intelligence are both progressive.

Figure 3-1, The Emotional Spiral, shows emotional progression in golf on the left side and emotional progression in leadership on the right side. Self-awareness determines whether the person will make a positive, upward movement in the spiral or a downward, negative movement. This results in a correspondingly positive or negative experience.

The model shows that, in the game of golf, with a reasonable level of self-awareness, a person has the opportunity to progress upward, gaining confidence and emotional momentum to reach the zone of peak performance for an athlete. If the golfer lacks self-awareness, it's probable that they will follow the path downward on the left side of the spiral, leading to confusion, frustration and anger, and have little performance excellence.

With self-awareness, leaders have a great opportunity to forge their way up the spiral. They can direct their own responses, connect with others and build quality, sustainable relationships. The leader whose emotions spiral upward establishes a positive emotional climate. The organization benefits from their work and they perform to their capabilities.

In the bottom right part of the spiral, the leader who lacks self-awareness struggles to direct their own responses, has difficulty connecting with others and experiences problems sustaining relationships. This is a disaster for the organization. The leader is ill-prepared to handle the challenges of leading others and creates a toxic environment in the workplace.

Visualize yourself in the spiral. Whether you are working, playing, parenting or driving your car, your emotions are always spiraling up or down, depending on how you direct your responses to your experiences. Your level of self-awareness begins the chain of progression and determines whether you spiral up or spiral down, creating positive or negative environments for others.

Self-awareness is more elusive than you may think

Among the people I work with, about 25 percent have a sufficient level of self-awareness to be a consistent top performer in leadership, sales, athletics or life in general. Now, I work with very smart, talented people who are in senior positions in their organizations or who are extremely talented in their field of endeavor. So, a quick calculation tells us that, at a minimum, about 75 percent of the population is not dialed in to their own emotions, and is not sufficiently aware of their strengths and weaknesses.

Figure 3-1, The Emotional Spiral

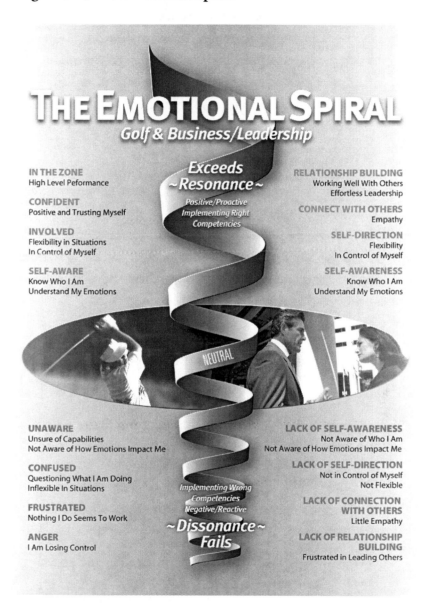

When I speak at conferences I offer a quick assessment tool to give people an idea of their self-awareness. Since the conference attendees represent a broad range of industries, they are good samples of the population at large. In this group, about 80 percent do not make the self-awareness grade. So, my analysis, based on my direct experience, indicates that about 80 percent of people are lacking in self-awareness. Most people do not know themselves very well!

Surprised? Do your own quick check. Answer the following few basic questions. If you can answer yes to every question, you might be sufficiently self-aware and able to direct your emotions upward in the spiral. If you cannot answer all the questions positively, chances are you lack self-awareness. Be as truthful as you can with these questions:

✓ Do you understand how your emotions impact you and your performance from moment to moment?

✓ Do you understand how your emotions impact others?

✓ Do you intimately know your strengths and limits? Can you write them down?

✓ Are you always honest with yourself about your performance?

✓ Do you solicit ongoing feedback from others about your performance?

✓ Do your actions always align with your values and goals?

✓ Do you make time for self-reflection and thoughtfulness?

How did you do?

As I mentioned in Chapter 1, our world is essentially upside down. Developing technical skills and cognitive abilities is always the priority. Being aware of yourself and developing your emotional intelligence is not. Most of us have never received any education on this subject and have never even questioned how our emotions might impact our performances day to day. Without provocation, how many of us would think about who we are, what drives us, our values, our strengths and limits, how our emotions may be impacting our effectiveness, how we impact others? And why would we want to ask someone for feedback that may not be flattering? The answers to these questions are crucial to your development as a contender and provide a foundation for moving forward with your life.

The following quote is from Dennis Waitley, author of The Psychology of Winning. I have set each statement apart from the others because I believe each of his points is immensely important:

> Winners have learned to know themselves intimately.
>
> They have learned to see themselves through the eyes of others.
>
> They have learned to feel as one with nature and the universe.
>
> And, they have learned to be aware of time—thus opportunity to learn from the past, plan for the future, and live as fully as possible in the present.

If you want to win consistently, a foundation in self-awareness is a must.

Let's look at some key characteristics of a pretender and of a contender, and see each of them in action.

4 Woulda, shoulda, coulda: pretender at the helm

"We live in a time in which most people believe there is not much inside them, only what teachers, parents, and others have put there."

Michel Cassou and Stewart Cubley
Life, Painting and Passion

From our talks, my caddie Brian could tell I was frustrated from a long, unsuccessful year and there were all sorts of things bothering me on the golf course, most of them beyond my control. When I would get in a bit of trouble, or start ranting and raving about something I could do nothing about, he would, in a calm voice, point out the futility of complaining about the weather or the state of the rough, and get me to focus on my routine and my game.

I had been letting small things bother me on the golf course for a while, and I would carry them with me through, not only a number of golf holes, but an entire tournament. That lack of focus was showing up in my results. Although I didn't know it at the time, my caddie was enforcing the 90-second rule with me. After a poor shot, bad break or anger at something way beyond my control, Brian would cut in almost immediately and get me back on track and focused on hitting the next shot.

Before I help you understand a few key areas of self-awareness, and what contenders do, let's take a look at what shapes a pretender and how a pretender acts.

It starts early

Confidence is in all of us, but how and whether it comes through or stays hidden depends on how we are treated as young people. How your parents, coaches, supporters and mentors treated you and spoke to you has a great impact on how you feel about yourself later in life. Author Jack Canfield tells us the average child hears 432 negative statements per day compared to 32 positive statements. And, research by the California Task Force for Personal and Social Responsibility tells us that only 20 percent of children and adults are able to handle put-downs without emotional pain or psychological damage.

So for the performer, a negative environment in the early years can have lasting effects. The child who was continually criticized will place far too much emphasis on his or her shortfalls later on. The child who was not encouraged to make their own decisions struggles to make decisions as a performer. If parents and supporters don't fully believe in a child in the early years, how can the performer expect to believe in him- or herself later on?

All of these negatives manifest themselves later on in a variety of ways.

Getting the boot: negative self-talk

I can remember myself and my playing partners in professional golf attacking our own confidence by becoming personal with our self-criticism. Instead of critiquing only our performance, we chose to attack ourselves personally with negative comments like "I can't believe how stupid I am!" "I can't do this. I'm going to quit this game. I'm no good." and "I'm a loser." You could hear all of these statements as we dealt—poorly—with the ups and downs of a difficult game. When the pressure was on and we started to struggle, these expressions started to surface. Our direct personal attacks went beyond performance assessment. Instead of attacking our missteps or errors by saying things like, "I bailed out on that shot," or "I lost focus," we were attacking ourselves as individuals, denigrating our own self-worth. Each of us tapped into our negative self-image and reinforced our beliefs about ourselves. This had a terribly detrimental impact on our actions. We were shaking our own confidence. With self-talk like that, who needs enemies? Self-aware performers do not sabotage their own performance!

Too high, too low:
set the bar where you can't reach it—yet!

It has been my experience working with people who describe themselves as being low in self-confidence that these performers will deliberately not set the bar high in life for fear of failing. And, not aiming high, they get average results. These results fuel their low confidence and the cycle of the self-fulfilling prophecy continues.

You must also be careful not to set the bar so far beyond your capabilities that you can never reach it. This also undermines your confidence.

I have found with my clients in different performance areas that setting the bar high enough to stretch your capabilities is a great place to be. You can then adjust the bar upward from this level over time as your abilities and confidence increase.

Temptation beckons

While contenders have emotional discipline, pretenders can be prisoners to their emotions and respond to immediate urges. They cannot resist the endless temptations of short-term gain. Lacking self-awareness, pretenders like to be comfortable. They start something for a while but after a short time come back to their point of balance—the point at which their performance goals match their skills—a point that is, therefore, comfortable and easy for them.

How about you? If you value something, and have the talent, will you stick with it? Do you start a project for a few weeks, and then when it becomes difficult, do you submit to negative emotions like frustration and confusion? Do you have unfinished projects in your home? Are you a collector of hobbies, buying everything you need but not following through?

Contenders' self-awareness and emotional discipline enable them to work hard at their craft and know what to practice to achieve the most benefit. Pretenders will work hard, but often the quality of the work is poor and the emphasis is on the wrong things. When I hit the practice area for the first time in Victoria, for example, I wanted to work only on my strongest ability, driving the ball. It took an intervention by my caddie Brian to get me to focus on putting, the real need to meet the challenges of the golf course I would be playing in that tournament. Like all pretenders, my intention was great but I lacked the self-awareness and emotional discipline to target the right areas.

Not having emotional discipline can cause irreparable damage. We see it often in business where the temptations of bigger gains are ongoing. It was widely reported in recent years that many executives in the financial sector succumbed to greed for their own personal gain at the expense of long-term company and shareholder value. You have probably also seen in the media how these executives and others paid themselves millions in spite of poor company performance. These undisciplined actions, far away from the core values of true contenders, caused millions of job losses, a stock-market meltdown, the failing of financial institutions, and a devastating credit crunch. This is the danger when pretenders are at the helm.

Pretenders don't want to know

Because it is important for contenders to understand other perspectives on their behavior and performance, they ask for feedback. I find something very interesting when I work with corporate groups. Often I'll assess groups of leaders or executives and without fail, high performers always request more feedback and want to know how they can get better. Lower performers shy away from feedback and are satisfied with the assessment results, even if they are well below par. Contenders can't get enough feedback to improve themselves. Pretenders seem to be happy with the way things are and just don't want to know about issues or problems.

I can remember in my golf career not really wanting to acknowledge a poor performance. It was just too difficult and too much work to relive an uncomfortable experience. I figured if I ignored it and swept it under the rug, it would go away, change by itself and never come back. Unfortunately, I was wrong.

We all need a coach, mentor, colleagues, friends and family members who can tell us the truth and give us valuable feedback. Pretenders don't ask for help, listen to feedback or adjust what they are doing in response to others' input. Instead, they have only one, biased perspective—their own. Without a high level of self-awareness, that perspective is usually very different from that of others. We all do need our own perspective of the world, but we also need the perspective of others to balance our personal views.

Drowning below the surface of awareness

There are countless examples of leaders who fail because they don't have enough feedback. How they are behaving is beneath their awareness. A high profile example is former Disney CEO, Michael Eisner, who flamed out after his great early years at Disney, during which the stock price soared and investors were delighted with Mr. Eisner's results. But during his tenure, Mr. Eisner made certain that Disney's board and executive group were filled with like-minded allies who would not be quick to challenge his decisions and performance. He therefore may not have had the feedback necessary to help him make a more positive impact on the organization. It did not end well for Eisner at Disney partly due to his inability to understand how he was being perceived in the company. Eisner is not alone. In my work I see leaders and performers every day who have sheltered themselves from critical feedback and, if they don't work toward self-awareness, the result is usually a path similar to Eisner's. The funny thing is that while these leaders will often say they are self-aware and believe it, their actions suggest something totally different.

Living up to others' expectations

Taking the advice of others to learn from one's own mistakes is one thing. Relying exclusively on the opinions of others to determine whether or not one has done a good job is quite another. This is another key difference between contenders and pretenders. Contenders set their own bar and are always trying to surpass it. They set their own standard of excellence; the bar is not set by someone else. Pretenders often get caught up in living up to others' expectations.

Professional golfer Greg Norman made a comment in Men's Journal Magazine several weeks before The Masters golf event in 2009. Norman was speaking about reasons why he never reached his enormous potential as a golfer. He explained:

> "Golf is a simple game. But I complicated it by turning people's expectations on myself."

We can all fall victim to this. Living up to others' expectations creates negative feelings.

Pretenders are often motivated by external factors like money, status, impressive titles or being a part of something prestigious. For contenders the external rewards are always secondary.

Releasing the burden of stress

Let's face it, we all experience stress in our day to day lives—some more than others. Sometimes a little bit of stress can challenge us and be invigorating, while a lot of stress can trigger a flood of powerful negative emotions including frustration, anxiety and anger. In most endeavors in life we must bounce back quickly because life offers us minute to minute challenges. Whereas contenders can unburden themselves from these emotions and move forward, pretenders may remain trapped in the negative emotions after the events that caused the stress have passed.

In addition, pretenders are less aware of their own negative emotions and the effects these can generate. These emotions therefore tend to stick around too long, build up, gain momentum, erupt and hinder performance.

The downward spiral

The career and behavior of golfer John Daly is a great example of someone who has succumbed to the pressures that being a champion can bring. When pressure brings negative emotion to the surface, Mr. Daly's apparent lack of awareness of his own negative emotion makes bad situations worse. Mr. Daly has traveled through tremendous peaks and valleys in his career. He is one of the top natural talents in professional golf, with great physical skills. He has won two major golf championships but his career has been marred by tremendous inconsistencies. His up and down professional and personal life is well documented in the media.

Daly is a great example of someone whose emotional triggers seem to be beneath his awareness. No one really knows, perhaps even John himself, what he is going to do when the heat is turned up and the walls start closing in. This has caused great harm to his career.

In the 1997 PGA Championship Daly tossed his driver in anger over a fence on the twelfth hole after a poor tee shot. The following day, in the final round, he got into an argument with a rules official over a ruling.

The most famous of his outbursts was in the 1999 U.S. Open, where Daly was unhappy with the hole positions set by the United States Golf Association. On the eighth green on the final day, Daly hit a short shot onto the green. After the ball hit the putting surface, it began to roll back down the hill toward him. Before it reached the bottom of the hill, Daly angrily smashed the ball one-handed to the other side of the green, upset that the ball did not stay on the green. He proceeded to finish the hole with an 11 and an eventual 13-over-par score of 83 on the day. He stated that he was upset with the USGA for setting hole positions that he perceived to be unfair. In one short expression of anger on the course he ruined his chances for any possibility of a good finish in the event. He also upset himself for something that was totally outside of his control.

You are in control

Mr. Daly is just one example of someone falling into the traps set for us everywhere we turn. There are so many things in your life and mine that are far beyond our control. It is easy to give them more attention than they deserve. These emotional hazards awaken your negative emotions and get you spiraling the wrong way. Just think about the things beyond Daly's control on a golf course—almost everything! I can make a long list of the factors that he really can't do anything about: the golf course conditions, the weather, crowds, his playing partners, the rules officials, and where his ball ends up after he hits it. These things cannot be changed. Trying to control them sets off an automatic trigger for anyone's sleeping negative emotions. Daly could let those negative emotions sleep if he would focus only on the things he can control: his attitude, routine, responses to poor shots, his equipment and his game plan etc.

Mr. Daly has ruined many opportunities to be a consistent contender. His up-and-down career has reflected his emotional stability. Has yours?

Consider yourself or someone you know who blows opportunities because the volcano erupts at the wrong time. You've seen it often: the leader or boss who can't control themselves, blow up once too often, and lose the trust of followers and employees. How about parents who regularly blow up at children and can't manage responses when they feel the heat? These eruptions can create fear and distance in relationships and they can have great negative impact on the climate of the environment—at work, at home or in any setting.

The volcano at work

Think about a boss you have had who couldn't manage their reactions and exploded when the pressure was on. These responses lead to all sorts of problems in a business environment. Instead of wanting to take your issues and challenges to the boss, you slowly pull away and lose interest in communicating with them. You may let it go for a while but over time, it wears on you and you begin a conversation with yourself about finding a new place to work.

Leaders who blow up and worry about the consequences later create negative emotional climates where there is fear and mistrust. No one wants to communicate with someone when you know the experience is going to be negative.

Trigger-unhappy

Think about the person at home whose temper is triggered by major problems and who lets go unpredictable eruptions making things uncomfortable in the family environment. You are never quite sure what to say to them for fear that the volcano may erupt.

Inconsistency is the hallmark of someone who has not identified their triggers. While they can sometimes be good, when negative emotions pop up, they are not so good—even terrible.

The line between contender and pretender in performance is very fine, and competitions can be won by fractions of a point. Competitors have to be resilient and put the difficult times behind them so that they can capitalize on the opportunities that lie ahead.

Pretenders fear change

Contenders can change and aren't afraid to do so. Pretenders fear change and are slow to do it. They are like someone trying to dance to music, moving from side to side and back to front, but wearing a pair of cement shoes. A pretender is someone who stays stuck in the same place while the world moves by, their heavy emotional shoes limiting them from making changes, and their weak emotional muscles unable to overcome that burden. With this image, it is easy to understand why pretenders aren't comfortable when change is necessary. It is easier for them simply to believe that what they are doing is working well enough.

My brother Kevin Haime is one of Canada's top golf instructors and offers instruction to all levels of golfers. He often has golfers coming to him who are struggling with their golf swings and really want to improve. One of his biggest challenges is individuals' resistance to making changes. People become so comfortable with what they are doing, even if it isn't effective, that the introduction of something new is highly uncomfortable. They may work on the changes for a while, but they become frustrated and don't stay with it. Many explain to him that they are afraid to lose what they already have, even if what they have doesn't work and produces poor results!

Nortel Networks CEO John Roth was standing still while the technology bubble was bursting. Once Canada's technology giant, the company is now in bankruptcy, with a stock price that couldn't buy a candy bar. The stock has dropped from $147 to its current 28 cents. Roth and his team were unable to deal with the unprecedented changes and subsequent downturn in their business. Back in 2000, they had purchased a number of companies with the bill totaling $19.7 billion US. These purchases went sour when the bubble burst. Unable to adapt to the failing market, the wheels slowly came off. The company went through three CEOs and became the subject of a number of criminal investigations around accounting practices. Nortel Networks is now hanging by a thread.

I've learned how important it is to help individuals recognize that change is almost always required. I help them build the emotional muscle needed to have the flexibility to adapt to change. With globalization, an abundance of competitors entering the market, and evolving technology, business changes so quickly these days that the ability to recognize the need for change, and then be flexible in the changing environment, very much separates contenders from pretenders. In sports, technology is improving equipment and requiring changes in technique, and good performers have to adjust constantly just to keep up. Because change is a constant in all endeavors it takes increasing effort over time to contend for great achievement. Complacency is death in performance. Let's look at the characteristics that enable contenders to embrace change and bring their performances to life.

5 Dance like a butterfly—the nimble moves of a contender

"Please ... tell me who you are and what you want. And if you think those are simple questions, keep in mind that most people live their entire lives without arriving at an answer."

Gary Zukav
Author, The Heart of the Soul

When the golf tournament began in Victoria, Canada on Thursday, I was ready—and so was my caddie, Brian. My anxiety and nervousness before the first round were there as usual, but Brian eased the tension with a funny story about his family as we walked down to the first hole.

In tournaments in the months preceding this one, uncertainty and anxiety were real problems for me as my confidence was low and I was frustrated. Brian knew this golf course very well, but it also seemed that he was getting to know me. When I started to dip down in the valley after a poor shot or some bad luck, Brian reminded me that things would balance out and that I needed to keep moving forward. Not only did Brian learn about my golf game during the practice rounds early in the week, but he learned about my habits and my character, and he had some useful things to say when I needed help.

By the middle of the week, Brian knew all of my tendencies and directed me toward my strong points. He knew my strength in golf was the tee shot, especially with the driver, so he helped me take advantage of that whenever the opportunity was there.

There are great performers who are excellent models of contenders in a variety of disciplines, including the game of golf. Self-awareness contributed to their ability to get to the top of the leaderboard in their sport or profession, and despite the obvious differences in the nature of the challenges they face, they share attributes that make them consistent performers and true contenders.

Contenders are in alignment

Contenders are in complete alignment with their values and goals, and their actions reflect that fact. They are motivated performers who will do what it takes and stick with it, to reach their goals.

Contenders know what their values and goals are. It has been fascinating to me in my work with great performers to find that many of the top ones have written down their goals in a very clearly defined way, including timelines. What are your values? Your goals? Could you write down your values and goals if asked?

Emotional discipline

Self-aware performers are able to focus on their long-term objectives and resist the endless temptations of short-term gain. Contenders have emotional discipline. Being self-aware is a key factor in this picture. Since contenders are aware of their emotions, they can manage negative ones, always keeping the long-term goal in mind and staying true to what they believe in.

Contenders work hard at their craft and seem to have a knack for practicing the things that will give them the most benefit. Because they are self-aware, they know what truly requires extra effort on their part, and they have the emotional discipline needed to practice those things. Knowing their strengths and limits, they target their practice on areas that require attention, and maximize their results.

Pushing the point of balance forward

Contenders shift their point of balance—the performance point that is comfortable and easy for them—to align with their long-term goals and ambitions. They push themselves. They know that to sustain performance over time, they must have the self-discipline to do what it takes to get there. Their actions are in complete alignment with their values and goals and they know what it will take to get to where they want to be.

I had the pleasure of playing golf a number of times with Craig Parry, the successful Australian golf professional, on the Canadian, Australian and Asian tours. I was always astonished at how Craig could compete at the professional level. He was about five foot four and shaped like a little round ball. He had a very funny swing that looped from inside to out and looked off balance in the finish. The thing I didn't know and couldn't see was that Craig knew where he was going. Before these events, I would often see him practicing in a vacant field for hours, and he spent endless additional hours working on his putting, a key part of professional golf. Beyond his preparation, I remember him being aggressive on the golf course, never playing for second place. In fact, when we played in competition, he mentioned my cautious style to me a number of times and always jokingly asked, "What are you playing for? You gotta go for the win, mate!" He also took the time to have fun with his Australian buddies and get away from the game. Parry was committed to his craft, was passionate about it, and was willing to do what it took to make it over the long haul.

Proportionally, it is interesting to note how many Australian golfers are successful and continually able to move their point of balance forward. I believe this is because they set out only to be professional golfers, and are wholly committed to it for the long term. This total commitment gives them the emotional discipline to work hard and press on through difficult times. Americans, Canadians and others, on the other hand, are often the products of American universities, and have fall-back plans if the experience of professional golf becomes too difficult and uncomfortable. Because they have a Plan B ready to go if things don't work out, their urgency to move their point of balance forward is not as great as the Australians'.

Warren, Bill and Tiger stay true to their values

Think about a contender like Berkshire Hathaway leader Warren Buffett who is always steadfast in his investing values and goals.

Over the years, the market goes up and down, industries like technology get hot and cool off, but he remains committed to his principals. He's in it for the long haul and does not get caught up in the emotional temptations of the market.

Another steadfast leader, Bill George, in his days as CEO of the medical devices company, Medtronic, was able to establish a values-based organization. In a survey of company employees, 87 percent of responders aligned their personal values with the values of the company. It's no secret that the company thrived, and with these values, became world-class.

In golf, Tiger Woods is well known for having the records of golf's all-time winner, Jack Nicklaus, on his wall when he was growing up. It was Woods's goal to one day break the all-time records, and he is well on his way to doing it. Woods's work ethic and routine remain as rigorous today as when he started. He has not been tempted by the fabulous riches that have come along with his success. He has continually shifted his point of balance, and with tremendous discipline, stays on track to reach his goals. His goal and values are rock solid, something that is true of all consistent performers.

Do you have the emotional discipline to stay with your goals and values? Are your values and goals always aligned with your actions?

Contenders ask others

Do you ever ask people what they think of your behavior? Do you consistently ask a coach how you are doing? Does he ask you how he is doing as a coach? Does your boss ask you how he is doing to help serve you better at work? Do you ask colleagues how you are doing? How about clients? It is a good idea to ask them what they think and whether they believe you are serving them well.

Contenders ask for feedback. They want to know how they are doing. It is important for them to understand other perspectives on their behavior and performance. In corporate groups of leaders and executives, it is always the higher performers who request more feedback and who want to know how they can get better. Contenders feel that they can never get enough feedback to improve themselves.

Feedback is one of the primary ways for us to understand our strengths and limits. Contenders intimately know what they do well and where they are limited. This is crucial under pressure, because it is when the pressure is most intense that weaknesses are exposed. I learned this the hard way in my professional golf career when I had opportunities to win and my weakness was exposed at the worst possible time, coming down the stretch. The problem was that I had never identified my strengths and limits and therefore did not have a plan to address them. While I believe, through my work with top performers, that working on strengths and playing to them is important, I have also found that you must make your limits serviceable. If you have limits that are your secret and unacknowledged Achilles heels, they can easily be exposed under pressure, usually at the worst possible time.

Do you intimately understand your strengths and limits?

Bill George, author of True North and one of America's great leadership minds, believes feedback is critical to reaching one's potential and a key to being self-aware. George explains in a recent article:

> I think the idea of 360-degree feedback, where you get feedback from your subordinates and your peers, is the most valuable thing you can do. And if you take that to heart, and really try to incorporate it into your leadership, and listen hard to what other people are telling you, you can become a great leader. Most of those leaders who fail are ones that just refuse to listen to the feedback.

The leader who creates an open culture where people tell the truth to each other, sees dividends in the long run.

We all need a coach, mentor, colleagues, friends and family members who can tell us the truth and give us valuable feedback. A contender asks for help, listens carefully to the feedback and makes the necessary adjustments.

Do you ask for feedback to help you understand where you might need improvement?

Contenders are honest

Contenders look in the mirror and aren't afraid of what they see. Contenders make mistakes. But they make an honest assessment of what happened and what they need to do to move forward to where they want to go. Contenders aren't afraid to look in the mirror and ask: What happened? Where did I go wrong? How can I do a better job next time? What do I have to do to make sure this doesn't happen again?

Just think of the consequences if you don't look in the mirror, make assessments and ask yourself these things. Would anything ever change? Possibly, but the changes would be a random shift. You wouldn't know the reasons why things changed and you would be open to the same situation occurring over and over again.

The really effective leaders I work with admit to their mistakes, and their followers appreciate it. There is a good level of trust because these performers are honest. They confront failure versus not admitting when things don't work. I have found that leaders who admit mistakes to themselves and others connect to their people and have greater influence. Honesty generates high levels of respect from others.

A Tiger in the mirror

Let me give you an example of how one of the world's great performers is self-aware, looks in the mirror, and asks tough questions. Here is an excerpt from a media conference with Tiger Woods immediately following the 2007 World Golf Championship event, which he won. The week before this event, however, Woods had had one of the worst final day finishes in his career at Arnold Palmer's Bay Hill Championship in Orlando, FL. He shot an 8-over-par 43 on the final nine holes of the event and a final score of 76 for the day. Woods talked about the win and about his poor performance in the previous week's tournament:

MEDIA: Once again you've come back from less than a top-20 finish with a victory. What are your thoughts on that, the ability to come back from a disappointing performance with a victory?

WOODS: I think you have to analyze your performance and where you went wrong. Too many people are afraid to look deep down and look at where you made mistakes. That's not always easy to do, to be honest with yourself. That's something my mother and father always instilled in me and even to this day, sometimes it's difficult, but you have to take an honest look and have an honest evaluation of your performance.

MEDIA: You referenced earlier this week about how you sort of processed your play last week. I'm wondering whether you look at stats or do you just do this mentally?

WOODS: All I know is from my play. I go over each round, each tournament, evaluate it, look back on it and learn from it. I'm not that analytical on writing things down like Annika, [Annika Sorenstam, the former number-one female golfer] but I will take a hard look at myself, and try and figure out where I went wrong, and also where I went right so I can build on that as well.

MEDIA: Is that analytical approach, is that by yourself, is that something you talk to Steve [Steve Williams, Woods's Caddie] or Hank [Hank Haney, Woods's swing coach] about, or what is that approach?

WOODS: Yeah, I talk to Hank a little bit about it. Steve, as well. But deep down, I know exactly what shot I was trying to play, and what the conditions were and what I was feeling and thinking. They don't know, so I'm the only one who can actually, truly take a hard look at it and be honest with it.

MEDIA: Along those lines, is it more difficult to be critical with yourself after winning a tournament?

WOODS: No.

MEDIA: Is there something you can learn or is it just not necessary after a win?

WOODS: No. You can still pick it apart, yeah. But you know, that's part of … how are you going to get better if you don't look at it?

Honesty has been a valuable asset for Tiger Woods. At that time in 2007, he had finished out of the Top 20 twenty-three times in his career. Of those twenty-three times, he had come back to win an event the following week fifteen times. This is one of the separators between Woods and his competitors that always makes him a top contender. He learns lessons from past experiences and is completely honest with himself moving forward. This allows him to make adjustments and prevent similar mistakes again.

Certainly if one of the world's top performers can look in the mirror and evaluate his performances, you can too. This is one of the primary ways contenders separate themselves from pretenders. They are constantly learning from all performances, including poor ones, and using the information to get better.

Do you look in the mirror? Are you afraid of what you'll see if you do?

Contenders know their triggers

Contenders understand what makes them tick and what bothers them, their trigger points. This is the basis for understanding how your emotions impact you. When the pressure starts bubbling, are you aware of what pushes your buttons and throws you off your game? The problem is that these trigger points can be beneath your awareness. So unless you have a great idea of what may set you off, the volcano can erupt at any time.

There is no doubt, from my work with corporate leaders, that those who know their trigger points create environments of trust and communication in their workplaces. One of the primary roles of a leader is creating a positive emotional climate. Emotional composure can help to do that.

Consistent contenders understand their trigger points and know when negative emotion will suddenly rise up and cloud their thinking. Aware of the damage these harmful negative emotions can do, they make sure they know what's coming and create a plan to manage it. This gives them a big advantage. Their bumps are smoother and they trip themselves up far less often.

Do you know your triggers? If not, I'll help you with this in the coming chapters.

Contenders bounce back

Knowing your triggers can help with your ability to bounce back from difficult circumstances.

Life is difficult, we all know that. Our parents tell us when we are kids that if you get knocked down, you must get right back up. And that's great advice. Contenders who are self-aware are able to change the impact of a negative experience into a positive one. They are emotionally resilient and can bounce back. Contenders are able to unburden themselves from these emotions and move forward.

Self-awareness is again the key to helping you be emotionally resilient. If you can identify the emotion you are feeling, the opportunity to direct it appropriately and replace it with a positive feeling is within your control. This is exactly what contenders do. Like everyone, contenders experience negative emotions too, but they are aware of the emotion, express it, and direct their responses accordingly.

Consider the PGA Tour bounce-back statistic, which counts the number of times a golfer who has a one-over-par score on a hole, bounces back with an under-par score on the following hole. This demonstrates how quickly the golfer can put the poor performance behind them and get back on track. If you look at the statistics, you will see the same names from year to year. It is no coincidence that the world's top golfer, Tiger Woods, has led the category several times and almost always appears near the top of the list.

How do you bounce back from adversity? Are you able to put it quickly behind you and get on with your life?

Contenders get away from it all
It has been my experience that this characteristic of contenders is a hard one to get most people to commit to. We are all so busy in our lives that there never seems to be enough time for ourselves. At least that's the excuse we use to avoid self-reflection and getting in touch with our thoughts. Calming your mind and

understanding the concept of being totally in the present can help you become a high performer. It's no coincidence that the two contenders I believe we can learn a lot from, Tiger Woods in sports and Bill George in business and leadership, both engage in meditation practices. Woods is linked to eastern beliefs through his mother, who is of Thai descent, and Bill George has been practicing meditation since his early years in business. Both believe in some sort of practice that requires you to go inside yourself and reflect on what is important. This time with yourself, away from the demands and pace of the world, can clear the mind from the clutter that accumulates every day in our hectic lives.

Woods is a great example of a clear, calm mind. Without a calm and clear approach, it would be impossible for Woods to survive and maintain elite performance in his fish bowl of a world where there are so many demands on his time, where media are interested in every move he makes, and where distractions abound. But Woods is able to center himself and do what he does best with calm, clear thinking.

The present is the place for performance

Can you imagine how great it would be always to keep yourself in the present moment? How much stress could you avoid if you did that? No worries about what happened yesterday and no worries about new demands put on you at work, at home or wherever? Contenders like Tiger Woods know the importance of staying in the present moment. While Tiger shows negative emotion after a poor shot in golf, it is very rare that you will see him let those negative emotions affect the next shot. With Woods, the only important shot is the one he is hitting, not the one he has just hit or the next one he will hit. He learned the importance of this from his father, Earl, who is quoted as saying:

> "There is only now. You must understand that time is just a linear measurement of successive increments of now. Any place you go on that line is now, and that's how you have to live it."

The present is a much calmer place than the future or past. Our past stirs our emotional memory—good and bad—and our own perception of the future stirs our emotions, positive and negative. While the future is where our goals and future achievements live, we achieve them through living in the present.

Do you take time for self reflection, even a few minutes every day, to slow things down and gain an appreciation for the present moment?

Contenders set their own standards

The great Russian dancer Mikhail Baryshnikov said it best:

> "I do not try to dance better than anyone else. I only try to dance better than myself."

Contenders set their own bar and are always trying to surpass it. The bar is not set by someone else. This is another difference between contenders and pretenders; contenders set their own standard of excellence, while pretenders often get caught up in living up to others' expectations. Tiger Woods has said:

> "One of the things that my parents have taught me is never listen to other people's expectations.

You should live your own life and live up to your own expectations, and those are the only things I really care about it."

In an interview, Woods's mother was quoted as saying:

> "I always tell Tiger, you can't do things to please other people. It will waste your energy, and you won't be happy in yourself. You have to what is right for yourself. And on that, he does a good job."

In 2000, Woods achieved one of the best performances in golf history, winning the United States Open Golf Championship by fifteen strokes. This margin of victory is unheard of in a major professional golf championship. The golf courses in major championships are typically very difficult and it is unusual for one player to separate themselves to such a degree from the other players. But Woods ran away from the others at Pebble Beach in California for another major victory. Following the victory, Woods talked about how he was excited to win, but looking forward to making changes in his golf game to get better. Now, you wouldn't expect someone who just won a major championship in golf by fifteen strokes to talk about getting to another level. This just highlights how Woods is only competing with himself and has set his own standard of performance. I'm sure he heard over and over again about how this was the greatest performance in the history of golf and was asked where he could possibly go from there. But, aligned with the values and goals he has established for himself, Tiger Woods has continued to move forward with consistently impressive performances.

Contenders are primarily motivated by intrinsic rewards like playing to their potential, a burning desire to achieve their goals, and the joy of a great performance. They have a passion for the work or activity or whatever they are doing. For contenders, the external rewards are always secondary. As tennis legend and humanitarian Arthur Ashe stated:

> "You are never really playing an opponent. You are playing yourself, your own highest standards, and when you reach your limits, that is pure joy."

Following the 2009 Accenture World Match Play Golf Championship, one of the top events in professional golf, the Champion, Australia's Geoff Ogilvy, was asked if he was satisfied with where he was in professional golf and what he would need to do to move forward. He mentioned Tiger Woods and said that the reason no one is close to him in the game is because Woods could win professional golf tournaments when he was not playing well. No one else could come close to doing that. Woods's powerful motivation, combined with his ability to manage negative emotion like frustration when things don't go his way, enable him to contend and win even when he doesn't have his best stuff.

Think about your own personal excellence. Do you set your own bar, set your goals accordingly, and always try and reach them with passion? Or, are you wrapped up in others' expectations and chasing superficial, external rewards?

Contenders are chameleons

Contenders can change and aren't afraid to do so.

Picture someone light on their feet, moving around from side to side and back to front, gliding around with ease. The music is playing and their movement changes as the music changes. A contender can move freely, changing direction, modifying their movement to meet a demand or avoid an obstacle in their way. Contenders who are self-aware adapt and are flexible.

What you are doing may not be working. Self-awareness gives you the opportunity to understand that there are better ways to do something and that you need to adjust your behavior or plans to improve.

So what does a contender like Tiger Woods do when faced with an unexpected turn of events that threatens his success?

He adjusts.

In 2006 at the British Open Golf Championship in Hoylake, England, the conditions of the golf course became very fast and hard in July as a result of unusually warm weather conditions. The golf course is usually slow and soft because of the generally wet weather in that area of England. Tiger Woods adapted his strategy by hitting iron clubs almost all of the way around the 72-hole tournament. Woods recognized that the conditions of the course required brains over brawn and he was flexible in taking what the golf course gave him. Most professional golfers win on golf courses that suit their style of game, but, because he is consistently flexible, Woods wins on every type of golf course imaginable. He is always flexible and constantly adapting his game strategy.

Leaders must be flexible

Consider the example of the tech company, Cisco Systems, during the burst of the tech bubble in 2001. The CEO of Cisco Systems, John Chambers, saw Cisco's stock drop 86 percent, from $80 to just over $11 when the bubble burst. He realized drastic changes were required for the company to survive and thrive. He changed the organizational structure of the company from command-and-control to a more democratic structure. Chambers also shrank the workforce and the number of suppliers, and streamlined products. The company emerged from the difficult times more profitable than ever, outperforming rivals. Even so, Chambers admits that he did not move fast enough saying:

> "Without exception, all of my biggest mistakes occurred because I moved too slowly."

Cisco Systems is thriving and a world leader in their industry, thanks to Chambers and his leadership team, and their responses to changing circumstances.

Have you identified where you might need changes? Is there a better way for you to approach things you are doing in your life? Are you acknowledging what's *not* working?

Contenders play with confidence

How you feel about yourself affects everything you do.

Contenders are confident in their capabilities because they are aware of them. They believe in themselves and their abilities. Their confidence is built from all of the core factors of self-awareness we have discussed in this chapter. To be convincing and humble, confidence must be built on the solid foundation of these factors. If it isn't built on solid ground, confidence can be shallow and arrogant.

In a sixty-year study done at Stanford University by Holahan & Sears, and published in 1995, researchers followed one thousand high IQ men and woman from the early years of their careers to retirement. The study found that the individuals who were most confident in the early years were more successful throughout their careers.

Becoming aware

Now that you have an idea of what makes contenders tick, and the importance of self-awareness in the recipe, let's move forward together and start helping you build the foundation for being a contender in your life. The first step in doing that is taking an emotional inventory of *you* and understanding how your starting point and the events in your life up to now may be impacting your performance on the job, in sports and in life generally. When you understand where you've been—your experiences—and what might trigger negative emotion in you, you can live with freedom in the present and not fear the past or the future. Let's start on your emotional inventory. This is the source of the way you think about things and whether your perspective is positive or negative.

6   The source of positive thinking

"Feelings or emotions are the universal language and are to be honored. They are the authentic expression of who you are at your deepest place."

Judith Wright
Australian Author and Poet

Brian helped me immensely that week and it's no coincidence that it was my best result of the year. I started with reasonable scores of 71 and 68 in the first two rounds, to get into good position in the tournament. I slipped to a 75 in the third round. But before the final round, my caddie Brian inspired me on the practice tee with some insightful comments about what he thought had happened the day before. I went on to finish the tournament with my best round, a 67.

I can remember very clearly what Brian said to me on the first hole during the last round. "Just play like John Haime and you'll be fine!" That's all I did, with some additional guidance from Brian. This was one of my best efforts in what had been a very frustrating year, filled with a lot of underachievement. It spoke to the career that might have been, had I had a caddie like Brian, who understood my emotional needs and who helped me play to my strengths and minimize my weaknesses.

Destructive emotions have a terrible tendency to have really bad timing. They seem to pop up at the worst possible times and when you least expect them. I think you know what I mean. Things are a little difficult at work and you make them worse by getting frustrated at the worst possible time and say the wrong thing to a colleague. You're late for the kids' soccer game; you pile everyone into the car and start driving only to find the slowest driver in the country in front of you. As you get closer and closer to this car, the stress builds, your emotions get the best of you, and you let out a number of four-letter unmentionables—with the kids in the back. Or, you are playing a round of golf and on the last putt on the last hole, you get an unpredictable bout of nerves and your hands go in a funny direction ... and so does the ball.

Don't think you are the only person who experiences this. It happens to everyone and we often don't know why. It shocks us and makes it seem like another person is residing in our body for a little window of time and then disappearing. You know this feeling; you do and say crazy things and a short time later can't believe you did or said them. The gremlin that appears in your body at those moments is always there, just making its presence known when you least welcome the intrusion. The gremlin's name is your emotional memory.

An emotional memory has power

Let me give you an example of the power of an emotional memory.

In the 2009 Masters Golf Tournament in Augusta, Ga., Kentucky native, Kenny Perry, a wonderful golfer and winner of many professional tournaments, experienced the power of negative emotions—and the result was devastating.

Perry was two shots clear of every competitor in the field with two holes to go in the tournament. It should have been a lock for him to par the last two holes, be presented with the coveted prize—the green jacket—and begin the celebrations. But hold on. Perry missed the green with his iron shot on the seventeenth hole, leading to a bogey 5. His two-shot lead was cut to one. He then hit a poor tee shot off the eighteenth tee into a fairway bunker. From there he hit a relatively short second shot extremely wide of the green, on the left. These events led to another bogey 5, a tie with two other players, and a playoff for the championship.

The three players went back to the eighteenth tee to play another hole to decide the winner. Perry hit a beautiful tee shot on the first playoff hole, finding himself about 150 yards from the green. He was in a position to win the tournament if he hit the type of shot he had hit in the first 70 holes of the event. But things had changed with Kenny and so did the result. He hit an iron shot that under normal circumstances would have been simple, but this time ended up 20 yards short and 30 yards right of his intended target.

With Perry and one competitor left, the playoff continued on the tenth hole. Perry hit a good tee shot but this time his iron shot to the green landed 30 yards left of his intended target. He had now left himself a difficult third shot and again scored a bogey 5. The tournament was over for Perry, who stumbled to the finish with three bogeys and a par after completing the first 70 holes with only five bogeys. Perry indicated in the post-round media conference:

> "When it gets down to those deals, great players execute and the average players don't. That's why they are where they are and we're down here."

Broadcasters, who see this kind of phenomenon regularly, usually introduce the final day of a major sporting event by saying "If he/she/they can control their emotions today, they can win this." Indeed, it is true that performers who cannot control their emotions, can't win. This is where the problem lies with many performers. When the pressure is turned up and the situation is stressful, negative feelings like anger, anxiety or fear can manifest themselves and come roaring out. The impact of these negative emotional expressions can be devastating in performance at any level of leadership, business, sports, the arts and more.

Consider the musician or artist who requires a relaxed state and clear mind to interpret the music and is overcome by negative emotion at the time of a key performance. Negative emotions can destroy performance very quickly. The physiological response in the memory is what can rise up and interfere with your physical performance or muddy your thoughts. As renowned Psychologist Edward L. Munn tells us:

> The emotionally aroused organism is aroused all over. There is an overall interaction of receptors, muscles, internal organs, and nervous mechanisms, with resulting changes in blood chemistry, in brain waves, and in general physiological reactions.

And, Psychologist and Author of The Human Element, William Schutz explains:

> After many years of being all but ignored, the importance of body function to emotional states is becoming recognized more widely.

I was speaking with Angelo Boy, a psychotherapist, author and emeritus professor at the University of New Hampshire. We were talking about the idea of mind over body. Angelo's perspective, expressed in his book Golf Improvement through Emotional Intelligence, explains the mind-body connection in more detail:

> This phrase is accurate as far as it goes. But it does not go far enough. Certainly a clear mind can control the mechanical reflexes of the body. But what produces a clear mind? The performer's emotional comfort or emotional intelligence is the source. A more accurate phrase would be emotions over mind over body. This phrase is more accurate because one's thinking ability isn't created in a vacuum. One's ability to think well has a source; it comes from somewhere. The source of a performer's thinking accuracy is inner feelings—one's emotional make-up.

What connects your past to today? Biology

Your brain is divided into two parts—the thinking brain and the emotional brain. The emotional brain is more powerful.

The boss of the emotional brain is a little walnut-shaped part called the amygdala, an ancient section that protects you from all threats and stresses. The amygdala had a bigger role thousands of years ago when human beings were worried about their survival every day. Life was about eating or being eaten.

In our world of complex social realities, the amygdala can really get us into trouble by not knowing the difference between a hungry lion and your mother-in-law. The problem is we are living in a very complex, social world with a primitive brain. The amygdala senses everything you do and matches the experience with the information in your emotional memory.

Your emotional vault

The emotional memory is like a vault that holds every experience of your life. Every person, place and event of your entire life is recorded there. Your brain's frame of reference for future experience, it is where your past and present connect. Your emotional memory includes your physiological responses at the time of your original experiences. Your responses may have included anxiety, tension, increased blood pressure and other reactions associated with fear, sadness, joy and a variety of other emotions. These are the very reactions you will then experience when your brain connects a current experience with a past one.

When you have had a highly emotional event in your life, the brain captures the details of the experience including who, what, when and where you are, as well as the emotions you experience at the time. All of these emotional memories are stored in your data bank with an emotion assigned to them. When you experience them again, they will be expressed the same way. Here's an example: someone you had a conflict with turns the corner on the street and is coming right toward you. The amygdala takes in the information and matches this guy with recent memories and they aren't good! So now you have the potential for anger, fear, anxiety and other emotions bubbling to the surface. You get the picture.

The memories in your emotional memory bank are both short- and long-term but you only retain the strongest good and bad emotional memories. Those memories that aren't strong fade out. The people, places and things that have had the biggest impact on you are all there, ready to go, when new experiences are introduced in your life.

What's in the vault?

What can you do about your emotions getting the best of you and getting in the way of your performances and life?

You need to find out what information about you is stored in your emotional memory vault. There may be unexpressed negative emotions from childhood experiences, from events ten years past or from last week. Since self-awareness is all about understanding yourself, the information in your emotional memory vault can help you better understand what makes you tick.

It is likely that golfer Kenny Perry has unresolved emotions from past tournaments, which popped up at the worst possible time, when he was about to win a major championship. In fact, in the 1996 PGA Championship, a major golf championship, Perry came to the last hole with a one-stroke lead and bogied the Par 5 eighteenth hole to eventually lose in a playoff to fellow PGA Tour player Mark Brooks. Thirteen years later, Perry, in his media conference after the 2009 Masters loss, admitted that he never really got over the 1996 loss. In fact, he mentioned that he felt the same feelings in the Masters that he had felt back in 1996. Those feelings, unexpressed, planted the seeds of doubt by replaying the negative emotions he experienced during the PGA event. One little thought about the 1996 PGA tournament could have begun a flow of negative emotions, including hesitation, disappointment and fear that would have interfered with Perry's performance in 2009.

We're going to look at a few simple strategies that can help you keep negative emotional memories from spoiling things for you, but first it's a great idea for you to look at your emotional roots and the potential source of emotional breakdowns. These big, negative emotional events inside of you can manifest themselves in so many different ways and come out as anxiety, fear, anger, disgust or even sadness. Just think of a time when you were under pressure and your emotions suddenly got the best of you. During this time you may have found you had a difficult time settling down and regaining your composure.

Emotions must be expressed. If they are unresolved, they will find expression some way, usually when you are in a difficult situation. That is bad news for a performer who is under a variety of pressures.

Thinking about your past and understanding what big, negative emotional events may be unexpressed is a great way for you to put them where they belong—in the past. For any person wanting to be a contender in any area of life, this is a great exercise to isolate harmful negative experiences that may be throwing you off your game.

I'm going to help you create an inventory of some of the big emotional experiences of your life. This will help you determine the root cause of your negative emotions and enable you to express them. Once an emotion is expressed, you can be free of it. Once you have freedom from that emotion and that memory, the fear of powerful, harmful emotional memories threatening you at the wrong time will be reduced.

Let me ask you a question: A child comes home from school and you can tell they are extremely upset. Something has happened at school and it is bothering the child. The child is very quiet when they come in the house, they go immediately upstairs to their bedroom and close the door with authority. What do you do?

One parent might go to the child's room and ask them what happened. When this is done with empathy, it opens the door for the child to talk about it and this catharsis begins the healing process. When the child is allowed to tell a parent or trusted caregiver what happened, the exercise of being heard helps the child be understood and puts the incident in perspective. The child is reassured that things are okay and they feel much better. They move on and the experience is behind them.

In contrast, if a parent's reaction is anger: "What are you doing? Come here and do your homework," the child is cut off from any chance to express the emotion inside. They may fear talking to that parent because they think he or she will become angry again.

If a parent's reaction is to ignore the child, they may get a sense that they are not valued. Even if the parent's reason is solid—he or she is busy with an important phone call, or has to go out and attend to another child's needs at that moment—the child in the bedroom feels the silence. They bear the full weight of their emotion and, unable to resolve the problem, the negative emotion and the event that precipitated it take a spot in the child's emotional memory vault.

What you need to do with your old, harmful, unexpressed emotional memories is express them, like the child in the first example, to someone who is empathetic. We all have major conscious emotional memories that hurt us. I have them, you have them, we all do.

You must become—retroactively—your own good parent or supporter, like the child had in the first example above. You have to express the harmful, negative emotional memories you never had the chance to express. You are becoming a good parent to yourself by finally dealing with the harmful memory. You weren't able to do it at the time of the experience, but you can do it now.

There are a couple of options on how you can do this.

Sharing the experience with an empathetic person you trust can be a form of catharsis and allows you to be heard and hear the expression of your emotion yourself. The person allows you to express the memory in a safe environment, and that person, like the parent in the example above, helps you put the experience in perspective. Your empathetic listener should not evaluate or criticize your emotions, or be judgmental.

Another form of catharsis can be expressive writing. If you are inclined to write, you can express your big emotional memories by journaling them on paper. This also provides you with an opportunity to get the memory out. Research by Dr. James Pennebaker outlined in his book, Opening Up: The Healing Power of Emotions, details the benefits to mental and physical well-being of writing about both negative and positive emotional memories.

However you choose to express your big memories, here are some key things to think about when recalling the biggest ones. You are recalling:

Situations that stirred intense emotion …

… with your parents

… with teachers and in school

… with jobs, bosses, co-workers

… with friends

… in sports and with coaches

… in activities you participated in and the people associated with those activities

Ask yourself:

When was I the most hurt?

When did I feel the greatest amount of pain?

Who caused the pain?

You are recalling experiences that caused you intense anger, intense fear or any powerful emotion. Think very broadly and consider all the people who were close to you and how they may have negatively impacted you.

After you have spent time on this exercise:

1. Summarize the experiences that were the most profound.
2. Talk about each experience and why it was so negative for you.

3. Consider how these experiences may be affecting life for you today.
4. Identify any triggers that bring these memories back to you in your current life.

Take your time identifying what you believe to be your most profound negative experiences. Think about some great, positive ones too.

Take your time identifying what you believe to be your most profound negative experiences. Think about some great, positive ones too. The worksheet on page 88 will help you keep track of some of your profound experiences. I'd like you to include your key negative ones and a few big positive ones. To get you started, I've included an example in the worksheet from my work with performers in various areas, including leadership and athletics.

Very often the people I work with are talented with great technical skill. But when an obvious opportunity for success arrives, they hesitate and find it very difficult to take hold. They have a difficulty with success. You would be surprised how many people have this difficulty. The roots of this fear often stem from a parent or supporter criticizing actions of a child and continually focusing on the negative parts of their performance. You know this well in children's activities where a parent continually focuses on the child's weaknesses, shakes their head when the child misses or makes a mistake, or criticizes the missed opportunities in the car on the way home. This stays with the child later on and, when as an adult the opportunity arises to metaphorically score the goal or win the game, the criticism and the words "You can't do it" or "You don't have what it takes" emerge. Then, negative emotions appear and the person succumbs to them. The problem is the person often has no idea why this happens repeatedly.

Once you have identified and expressed these emotions, it's time to put them away so they can no longer be a threat.

A few simple suggestions for old, harmful emotional memories

I like several ideas in recent writings by psychologist Dr. Joseph Carver PhD, that can help lock profound negative emotional memories away. Dr. Carver's first suggestion is for you to change painful emotional memories and alter the content. If you've had people in your life that have caused you grief and pain, add humor to the negative memory and change the memory. If you had a boss when you were young that constantly scolded you and criticized you, imagine them as six inches tall screaming from a small box or shaking their finger at you in a baby diaper. Doing this, you are rewriting the memory and the brain will resave the memory with your funny additions.

Another suggestion for you is sending old, harmful emotional memories to the junk pile by labeling them and sending them away. Traumatic childhood events, bad marriages etc. can be filed in one box and labeled according to the time period. Labels like "painful years" can be used. When a specific emotional memory or file comes up, you think to yourself that it is from the box labeled "painful years" and not needed anymore. Putting emotional memories together decreases the emotional impact of a single emotional memory.

Profound experience	What did it do to you?	How do you feel it is affecting you today?	Is there a trigger?			
When I played football as a kid, my father would scream at me from the sidelines when I dropped or missed the ball.	He embarrassed me at the time and I felt like I wasn't trying hard enough, even though I knew I was doing my best.	Because I really tried in football and my father still yelled at me, today I find it hard to try new things. I am always worried that I will fail.	Whenever my spouse wants to try something new or asks me to get a better job, we end up in a fight or I go out for a while to avoid an argument.			

If you'd like a more powerful image of sending harmful, negative emotional memories away, imagine taking a shovel out to your backyard, digging a big hole and burying your old, harmful emotional memories in a place where they will not be found again.

The goal here is to manage the emotional portion of your memory. Expressing negative emotion, changing your emotional memories, and filing away or burying your big negative experiences, helps you to put the past where it belongs and gain control of the present.

Managing your triggers now

Once you've looked back at some of your old, harmful negative emotional memories, and filed them away as history, there are some strategies you can use to keep negative emotions in check and not let them interfere with your performance. We all have triggers, things that press our buttons.

Contenders and consistent performers are driven by positive emotional memories. It could be that they had the opportunity to grow up in the Peak as we talked about in Chapter 2, or they have faced their negative emotional memories and stored them away. Because they are self-aware they can also identify emotions as they happen and slow them down before they take hold. This is an important point in becoming a contender, so negative experiences don't control you and spoil extended periods of performance.

Daniel Goleman, in his book Emotional Intelligence, introduced the casual reader to the concept of the amygdala hijack. When the amygdala hijacks your brain, the emotional brain takes over the thinking brain resulting in a knee-jerk negative reaction and a flood of negative emotion. If you've ever been "so mad I couldn't think straight," you know what I mean. In this case, your emotional memory takes you back to the exact feeling created when the original remembered event occurred.

Remember the 90-second rule

There is good news though—this is where your awareness helps you. If you know what bothers you and you feel the surge of emotion coming on, you can slow things down, shift to a positive memory, and change your state of mind. The ability to notice what is going on as it arises, and to slow down before you respond, is a crucial emotional skill. Brain experts tell us that you have about 90 seconds before emotion really bubbles up. Once your memory is stirred and you remember the facts about the person or event, the emotional memory kicks in. The emotion builds over this 90-second period. So, remember that when you feel the negative emotion rising up, you have 90 seconds to do something about it.

This is all significant in performance and your ability to be consistent. Think about the athlete who gets a bad break, succumbs to the flood of negative emotions and lets the rest of their performance be affected by the bad luck. The leader, who hears something in a meeting he doesn't like, reacts to the comment and the rest of the meeting is unproductive for him and everyone else. Or, the parent who responds to a child's mistake and brings the mood down in the house for the rest of the afternoon. The point is that while some small amounts of negative emotion can motivate the performer, the inability to manage strong negative emotion will destroy performance. You read about the golfer Kenny Perry, who is a wonderful golfer and a contender in all parts of his life. But, the power of old, negative emotional memories can challenge anyone, and the effects are physiological and powerful.

Certainly negative emotions are a part of your life and make life the rich experience it is. Feeling sadness, disappointment and anger, and the spectrum of emotions you experience day to day is normal, enriching, and makes you human. You can also use negative emotion to your advantage when the timing is right. You may see it happen or may do it yourself: An anger-driven little pep talk can give you a kick in the pants and motivate you to higher performance, the stern voice that tells you you are capable of more. But it is when the voice screams out too loudly, and too often, or when emotional memories we have not expressed jump up and confound us, that our performance can be far below what we are capable of doing.

You have choices about how powerful negative emotions impact you. Now that you have a small idea how the system works, it's time to take control of your powerful emotional memory vault and your triggers before they control your performances and life. They are a part of who you are and part of the journey in more fully understanding yourself. Contenders take inventory of past emotional memories and give them expression. They understand their triggers, manage negative impulses and are able to create a positive emotional climate that helps them to reach their goals.

In the next chapter, I'd like to introduce you to your new best friend, who will guide you on the path to great performance.

7 Building emotional muscle

"A good caddie is more than a mere assistant.
He is guide, philosopher and friend."

Henry Longhurst
Author and Broadcaster

The support and attention I received from Brian was a big part of my success that week. His feedback and good timing made a significant difference in my play. I was a lot more relaxed off the golf course that week too, feeling I was more in control of what I was doing. It highlights what an aware, available and accommodating caddie can do for a golfer. Not only did Brian carry my clubs and direct me around the course but he was my emotional caddie for the week. And the difference between that week and other weeks was significant. The remainder of the year was average at best. The week with Brian in western Canada was the year's highlight.

I believe that, if I had had a caddie like Brian with me in every pro tournament, my professional golf career would have been very different.

The problem was I didn't realize it at the time.

I know through my own experiences and through my business, working with top performers and with people who are aware that they need to change to become top performers, that all kinds of performers can be their own worst enemy. We can be very hard on ourselves and often don't give ourselves the benefit of the doubt that we give to others. But it is also possible for you to be your own best friend. This is your choice. It means not defeating yourself by allowing negative emotions and thoughts to impact your game.

Because I believe in what a great caddie can do for you, from this point forward in your life, I am assigning you your own Emotional Caddie to help you become more self-aware and enhance your emotional intelligence.

Your Emotional Caddie may be the voice we are talking about in this chapter, an internal mentor who guides you. Your Emotional Caddie is a presence of your choice; a positive, aware, available and accommodating force that helps you on your journey to great performance. Create a character that has resonance for you. It may be someone who has had a very positive influence on you like a grandparent; a wise, guiding force in your life. It may be the image of a favorite teacher or coach. This character is someone who knows you extremely well and will call you out when you are not being who you are.

You can give your caddie a name, to make him or her more real to you. For my purposes, I am going to call your caddie Brian, both in homage to the caddie who helped me at a time when I needed support, and because that name just happens to be an anagram of the word "Brain."

On your path to consistent performance, Brian will lighten the load for you, ensure that your talent is able to shine through, and allow you to focus on your goals. In your journey to becoming more self-aware, Brian will help you establish the relationship between positive emotions and clear thinking. He will offer gentle reminders, give you feedback, and ensure you are managing your emotions to the best of your ability. He will make you more sensitive, to listen to yourself and others and hear what is really important. From this point forward, you'll have a supporting actor and a clear perspective. Brian will even out the bumps for you, helping you to become more consistent. And, over time, he will help you on your way to being a consistent performer in everything you do.

Brian will help you become familiar with who you are, where you're going and how you're going to get there. He will enable you to become who you really are, so you can have the freedom to live well and perform to the best of your abilities.

As a highly supportive mentor, Brian will gently guide you day to day. He is a great supporter, a friend, someone who is going to tell you the truth and offer you alternatives as you go through experiences in life. He will make you laugh. He knows your values, goals and strengths intimately, and he will use all the information about who you are to keep you on course as you navigate life's challenges.

You will invoke Brian's help when you most need him (or her, if your caddie is female). I will begin helping you prioritize key areas on which you'd like to work. You may choose to address only your most pressing issue, or you may choose to work on the ones you believe are the most attainable at this time. Brian will be there for you when you need him. A great caddie is always available but there will also be times when you won't need him.

Your path to self-awareness will take time. There are no tricks, shortcuts, quick fixes or fast tips to speed up this process. I would recommend three to six months to work on the issues that are most important to you. Remember that building your self-awareness is an ongoing process. The more you know about yourself and where you are going, the more effective you will be.

Your emotional platform

Let's start by creating some awareness and a plan to get you started. The plan includes getting to know yourself a little better and identifying some key areas of self-awareness you must address and commit to, so that Brian can help you day to day and put you in a positive state to handle your experiences.

Knowing your primary emotional platform—your values, goals, strengths, limits, triggers, control factors and a sense of your emotions as they happen—will strengthen your ability to respond well in situations and develop consistency in your performances.

Remember, contenders know where they are going. They have a plan. Your plan will include five parts and three actions.

The five parts of your plan:

1. Define your values and your goals, with an initial focus on the short term.
2. Describe your strengths and limits—the things you do best and the things with which you struggle.

3. Identify the things in your life you can control.

4. Identify the things (including other people) you cannot control.

5. List your triggers—the things that really bother you emotionally, and your responses.

The three actions:

1. Plan time for self-reflection, where you will focus yourself in the present, reflect on what is really important to you, and clear your mind.

2. Be honest, with yourself and others.

3. Get feedback and regularly ask others how you are doing.

All together, these five parts and three actions constitute your primary emotional platform. They are what makes up you. Once you assemble this information about yourself, you and Brian will then be prepared to go through your experiences together.

Your value commitment

First, I'd like you to take some time to think carefully about your values and goals. Brian will need this information to ensure that your commitments and vision are completely in line with your day to day actions. As I mentioned in chapter 2, How solid is your base? the actions of contenders are completely in line with their values and goals. In order to be a contender and be consistent, this cannot be compromised.

I'd like you to write down what is most important in your life—your values. This is critical information for Brian to make sure that all your actions reflect what you believe in. Your values evolve from what has happened to you in your life and are influenced by experiences from childhood, your parents' beliefs, your educational experiences, your friends and more.

Contenders develop a meaningful set of values and priorities. Once you define them, your values impact every aspect of your life. Living your values is a powerful vehicle to help you become an authentic and consistent performer.

Staying in line with your values can be difficult. Temptations can be hard to resist. In the past few years you may have read about how, in business, values are being compromised in favor of short-term gains. In the face of temptation, Brian will promote emotional discipline and help you stay on course.

Focus on aligning your values with your actions. As a very simple example, if spending time with your family is a big priority for you, ensure that your work schedule is in line with this value. I often see people with great intention in their values, but their actions in no way align with those values. Your actions express your values. So if you don't live the way you say you believe you should live, then you cannot claim that as one of your values. Your actions cannot be taken in spite of who you really are. Your actions are who you really are.

What do you most believe in?

What is most important to you in your life and cannot be compromised? Rank what is most important to you.

I will not compromise on these values, which are the things in life most important to me:
1.
2.
3.
4.
5.

My goals

You are a performer in most areas of your life, so you'll need to set goals in different areas. Leaders, business people, sales people, athletes such as golfers, and other performers need to identify goals in different areas of their lives. It has been my experience that contenders write down their aspirations. There's something about writing down thoughts on paper that connects you with them. Many contenders I work with write down their goals and modify them as time moves forward and their priorities change. Their goals are always reasonable for the time, and fairly detailed on how they are going to achieve them.

Let's keep it simple initially. I would like you to think about your immediate, short-term goals. After all, every big journey begins somewhere, and creating and reaching some shorter term goals will give you confidence for reaching bigger, more ambitious ones later on. Figure out where you'd like to go today and next month, and next year. The next decade will be your next steps in terms of planning. It has been my experience that if you attempt huge amounts of change right away, you set yourself up for disappointment. Small successes will keep you motivated and in the game. This is the approach used in the Japanese business community, at Toyota and other companies. They call it Kaizen, loosely meaning continuous improvement. This approach starts with small, manageable steps to allow you to work toward bigger changes later on. The gradual shift makes change much less overwhelming for you. So, keep a big goal on the back burner and focus on some simple goals first.

Think about where you'd like to go and write it down. If this format does not meet your needs, choose your best format, but write down where you want to go!

At work, my immediate goals, which are doable and within my control, are:
1.
2.
3.
4.
5.

At home, for my personal life and family, my immediate goals, which are doable and within my control, are:
1.
2.
3.
4.
5.

In my passion—as a (golfer, tennis player, runner, musician, …) _____, my immediate goals, which are doable and within my control, are:
1.
2.
3.
4.
5.

Your strengths and limits

One area that is vital to you moving forward as a performer in your life, seems straightforward and simple, but I have found working with a variety of performers that it is not easy for people.

If you are not yet self-aware, it is likely that you do not truly know the extent of your strengths and the depths of your limits.

Think about yourself or someone you know well. How often do you see someone playing directly into their limits or weaknesses? I see it every day with people in careers or jobs that absolutely do not suit them. They appear uncomfortable in the job and, as a result, do not excel. How is it possible to excel consistently when you are playing directly into your limits as a person? It seems that people often channel themselves right into an area that will guarantee mediocre results, and where they are ineffective.

As a very simple example, I always find it funny playing golf in team competitions with different people, to ask them at the beginning of the event what they do best. They identify their strengths but, more often than not, after I see them play, the skill they mentioned as a strength is most definitely a limitation. I see this trend in my work with a variety of performers.

I also assess corporate leaders, and the 360-degree feedback from those very close to the person (their manager, their direct reports, clients, peers, friends and others) is always revealing. Very often what the leader perceives to be their strength in leadership, is perceived as a weakness by others who know the person well and who have an unbiased perspective of their behavior.

So you must think very carefully about your strengths and limits, and identify what you do best and what gives you trouble. Sit down and identify what you are best at in different parts of your life at work, at home, in your sport, and in your favored activity. For the most part, your key strengths and limits will be applicable in all areas of your life. If you are a great planner and organizer, you will take these skills into everything you do. If you are a people person, you will take this into all areas of your life.

When you begin this exercise, and once you have identified your major strengths and limits, it is very important to ask for feedback from people that are close to you. Ask family members, coaches, people you work with and other respected supporters what they believe your strengths and limits to be. It is key that you have a well-rounded view of what you do best and where you might not be comfortable. This is an excellent exercise to help you get into the habit of asking people how you are doing. It's very important in all areas of your life that you ask others for feedback to get a well rounded perspective of your performance. Brian will ensure that you periodically ask for feedback from those around you.

To capitalize on your best attributes, and utilize them in your experiences, Brian must be aware of your strengths and limits so he can gently guide you to areas of life where you can be most effective.

My strengths

My key strengths are the things I do with ease and that help me excel:
1.
2.
3.
4.
5.

My limits

My limits are things I do that make me feel out of place and uncomfortable, and that hurt my performance:
1.
2.
3.
4.
5.

Factors you can't control—an emotional trap

Welcome to a very large emotional trap for many people. How many times in a day do you waste emotional energy or get upset over something that is completely beyond your control? Many things in your life are beyond your control.

Another role for Brian will be to be aware of what is within your control each day and what is out of your control, and manage your responses accordingly.

In golf, most of the factors that bother people are completely beyond their control. You'll see golfers cursing and shaking their heads over the weather, where the ball ends up once they've hit it, good or bad luck, the other players on the course, and a long list of other factors. Focusing on these factors can quickly put the golfer into a downward spiral that has a negative impact on their performance. There are things a golfer can control, and you can also control some things in your life. A golfer can control his or her own work ethic, the quality of practice time, preparation, routine, responses to good and bad shots, equipment and general attitude.

I'd like you to identify what you can control in different areas of your life and think about a few key things you can't control in each area. Acknowledge what you can't control, but the areas you can control will be your primary focus.

At home, I can control:
1.
2.
3.
4.
5.

At home, I cannot control:
1.
2.
3.

At work, I can control:
1.
2.
3.
4.
5.

At work, I cannot control:
1.
2.
3.

On the golf course (or wherever my passion lies), I can control:
1.
2.
3.
4.
5.

On the golf course (or wherever my passion lies), I cannot control:
1.
2.
3.

As you move forward in your journey toward self-awareness, Brian can help you focus only on those things you can control. If you are able to put less emphasis on the factors you cannot control, you'll notice a big difference in the consistency of your emotional composure.

Know your triggers

You have certain people and situations that press your buttons. We all do. You started thinking about your emotional inventory in Chapter 6, The source of positive thinking, and created some strategies to keep emotional memories from impacting your emotional composure. I'd like you to think about what really bothers you and what may cause negative emotions to be triggered inside of you. When you are aware of your triggers, you can calmly defuse them when they pop up. This is Brian's job, to know your triggers, to recognize the situations that may trigger a strong negative emotional response, and then quickly defuse the emotion. Remember the 90-second rule. Let Brian pull you back and give you a small window of time to calm down and respond appropriately.

What really bothers you? What are your triggers?

The people who often trigger negative emotions in me are:
1.
2.
3.
4.
5.

The situations that often trigger negative emotions in me are:
1.
2.
3.
4.
5.

Do you know what you are feeling?
Your emotions in real time

A key step in emotional intelligence and self-awareness is being able to identify your emotions so you can best deal with them when they arise. Understanding why you feel a certain way is critical to your ability to manage your responses, especially when you are under pressure and when the emotion is strong. Here's a little exercise to help both you and Brian to identify your emotions as they happen to you.

Complete the sentences below and connect at least one emotion with the statements. This will help you get in the habit of listening to your emotions. The key is to be able to understand the source of the emotion as it arises, so you can learn to manage your response.

Complete the statements below that apply to you.

Reading this book I feel
When I think of my future I feel
When I think of my past I feel
When I finish work each day I feel
Generally at work I feel
On the first tee of the golf course, I usually feel
When I hit a bad shot on the golf course I feel
When I compete I feel
Before a big occasion that means a lot to me I feel
When I am with my spouse or partner I feel
When I am with my children I feel
When I am under pressure I generally feel

Make time for self-reflection

From simple self-reflection to deep meditation, the purpose of any reflective practice is to unclutter your mind from the many thoughts that preoccupy you each day, and put you solidly in the present moment.

This concept is critical for any repeated actions, where calmness and clarity of mind can lead to consistency.

In Jon Kabat Zinn's popular book Wherever You Go, There You Are, he explains the key benefits of the practice of mindfulness meditation:

> To allow ourselves to be truly in touch with where we are already are, no matter where that is, we have got to pause in our experience long enough to let the present moment sink in; long enough to actually feel the present moment, to see it in its fullness, to hold it in awareness and thereby come to know and understand it better. Only then can we accept the truth of this moment in our life, learn from it, and move on. Instead it often seems as if we are preoccupied with the past, with what has already happened, or with a future that hasn't arrived yet.

All performers can relate to the concept of mindfulness in the present. Many performers live in the world of should be, might be or could be, and miss the moment they are in. Grounded in the present moment is where you must be.

An awareness of ourselves in the moment can greatly contribute to understanding how our emotions impact us, and can also sharpen our perception. Your awareness of your emotions as they happen will enable you to manage your responses and be more effective.

I recommend that you and Brian start off your journey of self-reflection where you feel most comfortable. There are a number of levels of meditation. Start with ten minutes every day, calming your mind, clearing out the clutter, and working to stay in the present moment. Over time, as you experiment with what works for you—and feels right—you can increase the time you commit to self-reflection and meditation.

The results of a lack of self-awareness

For Brian to be truly effective, he must have the true picture of you. This gives him the opportunity to build up your emotional muscles to deal with your experiences in the best ways, and allow you to perform effectively and consistently.

I have developed a model for you to get an idea of some of the results of not having self-awareness. In Figure 7-1, I highlight some negative emotions that can emerge out of a lack of self-awareness, from not knowing who you are. From these emotions, a variety of negative behaviors can also emerge. I have included a few on the outside of the circle. A lack of self-awareness can also lead you to create a screen or shield around yourself because you lack the awareness to deal openly with your experiences. This superficial shield prevents you from showing who you truly are. It also blocks you from achievement. Keeping the shield in place is emotionally exhausting. People who do this—consciously or not—do not have sufficient emotional strength left over for significant achievement.

Figure 7-1: The results of lacking self-awareness—The Superficial Screen

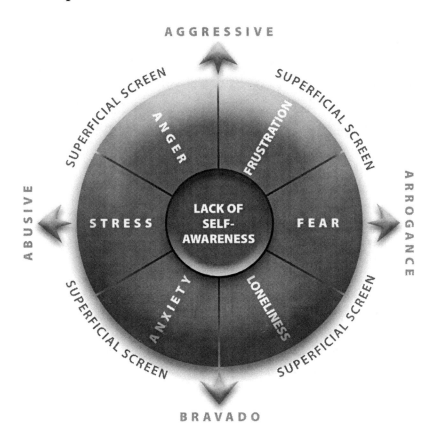

Now that you have the beginnings of a blueprint of who you are, it's time to put Brian into action. Since Brian now knows who you are, he can begin helping you build emotional muscle and nurture some key characteristics of a contender as you deal with your everyday experiences and challenges.

8 Strong and steadfast: Meet your new best friend

"Obstacles will look large or small to you according to whether you are large or small."

Orison Swett Marden
American Writer

Now it's time for your caddie to go to work. Brian now has a picture of you and knows who you are. Brian understands all the pieces that make you self-aware. He can now intervene between you and any experience in your life. You might think of Brian as your emotional bodyguard, making sure that the real you, the core of your self-awareness, is at the forefront in your experiences so you can respond to your challenges with flexibility, resiliency, honesty, confidence and a drive to achieve.

Let me introduce you to an image I've developed for you to help you visualize Brian in action. At the heart of Figure 8-1 is your self-awareness—information about you. You and Brian will use this information to deal with your experiences and challenges to the best of your ability.

Brian stands between the real, self-aware you and each of the experiences and challenges you face. Brian's job is to have who you are in the forefront and respond to experiences and challenges with the powerful behaviors of a contender. Brian will build your emotional muscle every day, by asking you questions on the best ways to deal with your challenges while being true to who you are.

In the illustration, the characteristics of flexibility, resiliency, honesty, confidence and drive to achieve are the primary tools Brian will use to navigate your experiences and challenges. As the outside area of the illustration shows, the ultimate result of dealing well with your experiences is consistent performance.

Think of Brian as your emotional muscle; he gives you strength whenever you veer off course or are not being yourself. He will ask questions for you to consider to get back on course. He is an ongoing reminder of who you are, your values, goals and strengths, and the key things that define you.

Let's look at the tools you will use to approach your experiences and challenges, and some suggestions on how Brian might help you use these tools.

Approach your experiences and challenges with honesty

Being self-aware is about being honest with yourself. From this point forward, you and Brian will be completely honest. You will look in the mirror following an experience in any area of your life and learn from it. As I mentioned to you in Chapter 5, Dance like a butterfly: the nimble moves of a contender, contenders like Tiger Woods look in the mirror, evaluate their performances and come back bigger and better than ever the next time. If you fail to consider this valuable information about yourself and your performance, you miss an opportunity and lose a life lesson and the learning that can come from it.

Figure 8-1: Your Emotional Caddie in action

Having the courage to ask others ties in with personal honesty. Feedback from others will help you define what needs work and what doesn't, so that you can improve your performance. Looking in the mirror will also help you expand your knowledge about your strengths and limits as you evaluate your performances and understand the sources of your mistakes and your achievements.

How your emotional caddie will help keep you honest

After any significant experience in which you feel you could have done better, Brian will be your reflection in the mirror, helping you to keep it real and asking the following questions:

What happened?

What did I do wrong?

What did I do well?

What do I need to do to perform better next time?

What do I have to do to make sure it doesn't happen again?

Asking these questions will keep you moving forward and help you take positive lessons from your experiences.

Approach your experiences and challenges with flexibility

The legendary golfer Jack Nicklaus often said that golf was about two things: emotions and adjustments. This statement could apply to everything in life. You must constantly make adjustments and adapt to situations you encounter, looking for opportunities to shift and change.

If you cannot recognize what might need a shift in your life, ask the people you respect to give you their thoughts on changes they believe you need to make to move forward and reach your goals.

It's going to be difficult for you to look for ways to change the things you do. We all get comfortable doing things one way and our perception is that the old way is the best way to do something. That's why you need Brian, to gently push you and encourage you to look at your experiences differently.

If you find yourself in changing situations, work on adapting your approach as the requirements of situations change. Remember, the very best leaders, business people, athletes, including golfers, and other performers are not afraid to change their strategy or goals in response to a changing environment.

What you are doing may not be working. A better awareness of yourself gives you the opportunity to understand that there may be better ways to do anything. Different perspectives and adjustments to behavior or plans are necessary for you to get better.

How Your Emotional Caddie Will Help You Become More Flexible and Adapt to Your Environment

Brian will make you aware of the potential need for change by identifying opportunities to do so. If what you are doing is not working, you'll need a push to help you look at things differently and consider what might work better. Here are a few questions Brian might ask you to help you be more flexible and effective:

Is there a better way for me to approach this situation? Can I do it differently?

Am I acknowledging what's not working? Why or why not?

What can I change to improve the situation?

What can I not change?

For example, if you are a leader, varying your approaches and leadership styles in certain situations or with certain people can have a great impact on your effectiveness. Adapting to the situation and any individual person can completely change the dynamic of the experience and the result.

If you are an athlete, think about how you can best apply your strengths in certain situations. A little change in strategy, to play to your strengths in key moments, can make a big difference in your results.

If you are struggling in certain parts of your career, consider what you may be doing to cause these struggles or what you could do differently to change your working dynamic with some colleagues.

Approach your experiences and challenges with resiliency

Contenders bounce back when the going gets tough. When they run into difficulty and experience a setback, they move forward and put the difficult experiences behind them.

Negative emotion lays beneath the awareness of the pretender and these destructive feelings can stick around long enough to do damage to your immediate future.

You build resiliency by understanding your emotions as they happen and having the ability to direct negative emotion. All performers go through ups and downs; it's a natural cycle. But contenders express their negative emotion and quickly move ahead to put a positive foot forward on the next golf hole, the next play, the next point, the next meeting or the next sales call. Contenders are emotionally resilient.

How your emotional caddie will help you bounce back

From this point forward, Brian will be there to remind you often that the 90-second rule is important for you to maintain good, consistent performance. When you are having difficulty, which you will, and you begin to feel negative emotions bubbling up, it is important that you recognize the emotion, express it in a responsible way, and put it behind you.

Whether the situation is big or small, whether the failure is significant or insignificant, Brian will remind you that the elements of your response must be the same:

1. Feel the experience.
2. Acknowledge the emotion.
3. Express the emotion.
4. Prepare for the next experience.

Here are a few questions Brian might ask you to help you to bounce back:

What went wrong?

Can I do anything about what just happened?

Will thinking about it help me?

What is my next challenge?

For example, the line is so fine at the top performance levels in business, leadership, sport and other performance areas that not immediately bouncing back from setbacks is very costly. If you allow a recent failure to affect your next opportunity, you will end up missing a series of opportunities that you cannot get back.

I found this often playing professional golf. Carrying forward the negative energy from a missed shot on one hole—sometimes for only one shot, or sometimes for the rest of the day—limited my ability to take advantage of my talent. I did this enough times during the course of some years to allow it to have a significant impact on my career. When I add up the opportunities I missed by worrying or agonizing about shots I couldn't do anything about—because they had happened moments or hours or days earlier—it amounts to a considerable opportunity lost to lower my scores in tournaments. If you are a performer, this is something you must avoid so you can maximize your performance.

As you develop self-awareness, your ability to stay in the present moment will help you become more resilient.

Approach your experiences and challenges with the drive to achieve

This characteristic of a contender ties closely to your values and goals. Once you have set your own clear, reasonable goals, it is up to you to maintain that standard and work towards it. Pretenders live by others' expectations and constantly compare themselves with others. Contenders passionately move toward their goals and are really only concerned with their own personal standards of performance. Contenders also always seem to have extrinsic rewards like income, status or impressive titles as a secondary goal. The passion to do well and achieve a standard of performance is the primary one.

How your emotional caddie will help your drive to achieve

You and Brian know your goals and values and where you would like to go. Brian will keep you focused on your own goals and not on what others might expect of you. And, most importantly, Brian will ensure that you are pursuing your goals with a passion to achieve excellence and not to accumulate superficial rewards.

Brian might ask you some of the following questions to help your drive to achieve.

Am I playing to the standards I set for myself?

Am I concerned about anyone else's expectations?

How hard do I have to work to achieve this goal?

Am I doing what it takes to reach my goals?

Am I shifting my point of balance forward as needed to achieve more?

Am I focusing on the process of the task and not the end reward?

I see many young athletes getting caught up in the expectations of others, including the dreams of their parents, supporters, teachers and others. These expectations confuse the athlete and put unnecessary pressure on individual performances. It is critical for the performer to have his or her own standards. These standards must be developed through the performer's passion to play and to develop their talent so they can get more and more enjoyment from playing at higher levels.

In the business environment, I find that some of my clients have lost sight of the reason they are working or why they chose to work in their specific area of expertise. The paycheck and moving up the ladder take precedence over their original goals. It is important to step back periodically, remember why you chose your work, and think about the importance of your work to others. When you enjoy what you do, appreciate how you might be helping others, and set the bar high enough for yourself in the position, the focus turns to process and performance and less to the extrinsic factors attached to the work.

Approach your experiences and challenges with confidence

Since you and Brian know who you are, you have something to believe in as you experience the challenges of your life.

Not only will you and Brian address each experience with confidence, but you will build your confidence by using the tools we have talked about in this chapter. Confronting your experiences with honesty, flexibility, resiliency and a drive to achieve will allow you to be more successful. This will, in turn, give you a stronger feeling that you can do it.

As you develop self-awareness, you will become more and more familiar with your strengths and limits, allowing you to play to your strengths more often, and putting you in a position to do well. This will build your confidence. You will have also set your bar at the right level when developing your goals, so you will not be reaching too high or too low. This will allow you to build your confidence slowly.

Because you have thought about where you have come from and what old, powerful, negative emotional memories may be holding you back from great performances when you are under pressure, you are now more self-aware. You have learned about yourself and are using some techniques and approaches that will help you learn more. Brian knows where you've been, where you have come from and where you are going. This knowledge will give you confidence.

Brian will look out for opportunities for you to act with confidence and to build your self-confidence as you achieve greater success.

How your emotional caddie will help you be confident

Brian will be sensitive to how you talk to yourself. Your new approach will be to talk to yourself as you would talk to your best friend. Brian will support you. Negative self-talk triggers negative emotion. Positive self-talk triggers positive emotion.

As a performer you will need constantly to enhance your skill sets so your capabilities are intact when it is time to perform. Brian will make sure you do the appropriate amount of work to build your skills. He will ensure you use your practice and preparation time wisely, and ask if you are being efficient and working on the things that will help you reach your goals.

Brian will remind you that, at this time, it does not matter what has happened in the past. With his inspiration, you will realize that every experience is a new situation and you will act with confidence. Brian will ask you how your strengths can best help you right now.

Moving forward with your emotional caddie

I think you get the idea of how the Emotional Caddie works.

You will customize your Emotional Caddie to best suit your own experiences and challenges. Remember that your Emotional Caddie is always there to support you. He or she is the emotional muscle between you and your experiences. You'll now have the security of knowing that if you venture off course, your Emotional Caddie will keep things real and ensure that you stay true to yourself. Life is challenging and we all need a helping hand. Your Emotional Caddie is yours.

9   Using your strength

*"Our deepest fear is not that we are inadequate. Our
deepest fear is that we are powerful beyond measure.
It is our light, not our darkness that most frightens us.
We ask ourselves, who am I to be brilliant, gorgeous,
talented, fabulous? Actually, who are you not to be?"*

Marianne Williamson
Author of A Gift of Change

So, where do you go from here? Or, should I say, where do you
and your Emotional Caddie go from here?

Knowing yourself, becoming self-aware and building emotional
muscle is a process. It is ongoing. It is not something you just
get, but something you work towards and slowly include in your
life. The shift from pretender to contender will be made during
this process. Be patient. The rewards are vast if you follow a path
to becoming self-aware and then utilize that self-awareness to
discover you and your true talents, ambitions and capabilities.

During the process of writing this book, people have asked me,
"Okay, so what's next? What comes after self-awareness?" "Where
do I go from here?" and "Where's the silver lining?"

My answer to all of these questions is ... living a better life is next.

Being self-aware and the great knowledge you now have about yourself gives you the freedom and power to compete, perform … and live your life. And if you live this life with passion and joy, and do it your way, what else can there possibly be?

You are utilizing your talents and abilities, free from destructive negative emotions, and you and your Emotional Caddie are taking advantage of the opportunities and experiences life presents. Every reader who reads this book will have different values, different goals, different strengths and a different path. You will be a contender in your own way—performing consistently and giving back as we talked about in The Emotional Peak in Chapter 2. You won't be Tiger Woods or Bill George or any other contender, but you will be an authentic version of yourself, focusing on the area in life where you can be a contender and make the most impact.

The doorway to performance

Being self-aware and using the tools you need to act accordingly, opens the doorway to performance in all areas of life. You now have the ability to connect with others, to show empathy and to develop quality, sustainable relationships in your life. A sufficient level of self-awareness allows you to regulate your responses and motivate yourself. Without self-awareness, people constantly struggle in relationships. This makes sense. If you don't fully understand yourself, how can you possibly understand another person?

Won't it be great to know yourself well enough that you can confidently connect with others in your organization, display empathy, create a positive emotional climate and lead them to great results?

Won't it be great to stand on the first tee on a golf course with no fear and hesitation, and play to your abilities with passion and without all the baggage you carried around to sabotage your performance?

If you are an artist or musician, won't it be great to experience the joy of the music as you play, without all the negative strings and with no worries attached? You will carry with you a flexibility to adapt to any situation that life throws at you.

If you want these results, it will require effort and a long-term commitment from you.

I can't guarantee that you won't be frustrated sometimes, but now you will have the tools you need to deal with the frustration and put yourself in the upward spiral.

Why I wrote this book

One of my primary motivations in writing this book was to respond to a need. Every day, I see so many people succumbing to the performance tricks, quick fixes and tips that are offered everywhere you turn, supposedly to make things easier. You can get a sense of this short-term fixation when you visit your local bookstore and see the volumes of books in the leadership, golf and self-help sections. People are looking for answers and there are lots being provided. But the answer seekers are only being satisfied temporarily and then it's back to the bookstore for the next idea.

While your life may seem different for a while with these solutions, there is an ongoing circle of failure and frustration. In a short time you are back to where you were and looking for the next solution. I had my eyes opened to it in the game of golf, in other athletic endeavors, and in my work in leadership, where all sorts of quick fixes are offered to address behavior. But the quick fixes never go deep enough to address root causes.

The chain of performance begins with your emotions and how you process the world. The chain progresses to your cognitive abilities. Then you act, and finally you have the results of your performance. So, to address the root causes of your behavior and why you do what do, you must address how your emotions impact you.

As I have told you, in my own professional golf career, I tried every trick, quick fix and tip, and went in circles trying to become a contender. My life journey led me to the realization that self-awareness and how you direct yourself in your experiences is the foundation for everything you need as a performer in any discipline: as a leader, a sales person, a golfer, a runner, a football player, a musician and more. It is a solid foundation on which to stand and it prepares you for any situation. It goes directly to the source—you—and enables you to use your talents to the best of your ability.

This has been my experience in working with great performers in all areas of life. Self-awareness and the application of honesty, flexibility, resiliency, confidence and a drive to achieve opens the door to accomplishment in anything you choose.

You gotta believe

I have focused most of this book on self-awareness, because without it, there is no moving forward. It is the most important tool in your toolbox and the foundation for everything you do. It is *the* fundamental characteristic of every contender, and consistent performance is impossible without it. Yes, you can have some good performances without being self-aware, but performing with consistency will not be possible.

If you look back at the foundation of the Peak model in Chapter 2, you will find that a common characteristic of the parents who create emotionally stable environments is that they believed in their children and gave these young people confidence to believe in themselves. They were the child's first Emotional Caddie, helping to build emotional muscle at an early age. There's nothing more satisfying in life than knowing that someone truly believes in you. This can enhance your own belief in yourself.

I don't believe I ever truly saw myself in the winner's circle when I was playing top level professional golf. Yes, I saw myself win at the lower levels of competition but when I arrived at the top levels, I don't think I knew myself well enough to have the self belief to consistently win.

While talent, hard work, working smart and preparing well are all requirements of a contender, these factors can only get you in the game. They will not make you a consistent performer. Many performers today work very hard and have the knack for working on the right things. But only a sincere belief in your abilities, originating out of self-awareness and solid emotional muscle, will take you to the next level. And that is why you need emotional muscle to be a contender.

A closing note to you

There are no secrets in making the shift from pretender to contender. If there were, I'd gladly pass them on to you. As you continue your journey and growth in getting to know who you are, and use this knowledge to direct yourself in your experiences, you will better understand why you feel what you feel and why you behave as you behave. That understanding then gives you the opportunity and freedom to make adjustments and live the life you want.

Like all great performers, you will re-create yourself many times over. As you struggle in the hills and valleys of life, as everyone does, being self-aware and knowing yourself intimately will give you the capacity to adapt to your environment, show resiliency and re-create yourself.

Knowing yourself and being self-aware is as basic and fundamental a concept to a human being as there is. But, as I mentioned early in this book, self-awareness is elusive and most people don't have it. You have the opportunity to develop it. If you understand yourself well, understand where you come from, understand how your primary connection to the world—your emotions—influences you, and work with your Emotional Caddie to build your emotional muscles, you have set the table to be a contender in whatever you choose.

About the Author

John Haime, President of LearningLinks Inc. combines the unique skills of someone who has played tournament golf at the highest levels and someone who has consulted with the world's top organizations. His skills help performers in business and sports enhance their performances and lives.

John's warm, engaging style, formative experiences on the world stage of golf, and practical approach enable him to help performers in all areas of life become masters of their own game.

He lives in Ottawa, Canada with his wife and son.

To connect with John with questions or comments, please visit www.learninglinks.org or www.newedgeperformance.ca.

References

Boy, Angelo, (2007). Golf Improvement through Emotional Intelligence. Baltimore: Publish America.

Carver, Joseph, (2009). Emotional Memory Management: Positive Control Over Your Memory.

Cooper, Robert, (1997). Executive EQ. New York: Berkley Publishing Group.

George, Bill, (2007). True North. San Francisco: Jossey Bass.

Ellis, Albert, (1975). A Guide to Rational Living: Wilshire Book Company.

Goleman, Daniel, (1995). Emotional Intelligence. New York, NY: Bantam Books.

Goleman, Daniel, (1998). Working with Emotional Intelligence. New York: Bantam Books.

Haime, John, (2004). On-Course Coaching. Pages 18-61.

Kabat-Zinn, Jon, (1994). Wherever You Go There You Are. New York: Hyperion.

Newman, Martyn, (2007). Emotional Capitalists. West Sussex: John Wiley & Sons.

Pennebaker, James, (1997). Opening Up: The Healing Power of Expressing Emotions. New York: Guilford Press.

Rogers, Carl, (1980). A Way of Being. Boston, MA: Houghton Mifflin.

Rogers, Carl, (1995). On Becoming a Person. New York, Mariner Books.

Salovey, P. & Mayer, J.D., (1990). "Emotional Intelligence": Imagination, Cognition and Personality.

BUY A SHARE OF THE FUTURE IN YOUR COMMUNITY

These certificates make great holiday, graduation and birthday gifts that can be personalized with the recipient's name. The cost of one S.H.A.R.E. or one square foot is $54.17. The personalized certificate is suitable for framing and will state the number of shares purchased and the amount of each share, as well as the recipient's name. The home that you participate in "building" will last for many years and will continue to grow in value.

Here is a sample SHARE certificate:

YES, I WOULD LIKE TO HELP!

I support the work that Habitat for Humanity does and I want to be part of the excitement! As a donor, I will receive periodic updates on your construction activities but, more importantly, I know my gift will help a family in our community realize the dream of homeownership. **I would like to SHARE in your efforts against substandard housing in my community!** *(Please print below)*

PLEASE SEND ME _____ SHARES at $54.17 EACH = $ $_____

In Honor Of: _____

Occasion: (Circle One)   HOLIDAY   BIRTHDAY   ANNIVERSARY

       OTHER: _____

Address of Recipient: _____

Gift From: _____ *Donor Address:* _____

Donor Email: _____

I AM ENCLOSING A CHECK FOR $ $_____ PAYABLE TO HABITAT FOR HUMANITY _OR_ PLEASE CHARGE MY VISA OR MASTERCARD *(CIRCLE ONE)*

Card Number _____ Expiration Date: _____

Name as it appears on Credit Card _____ Charge Amount $ _____

Signature _____

Billing Address _____

Telephone # Day _____ Eve _____

PLEASE NOTE: Your contribution is tax-deductible to the fullest extent allowed by law.
Habitat for Humanity • P.O. Box 1443 • Newport News, VA 23601 • 757-596-5553
www.HelpHabitatforHumanity.org

CPSIA information can be obtained at www.ICGtesting.com
Printed in the USA
LVOW080926091211

258497LV00004B/1/P